Wall Street

Wall

YALE UNIVERSITY PRESS   NEW HAVEN & LONDON

Street

America's

Dream Palace

Steve Fraser

Published with assistance from the foundation established in memory of Philip Hamilton McMillan of the Class of 1894, Yale College.

Set in Janson by Integrated Publishing Solutions.
Printed in the United States of America.

The Library of Congress has cataloged the hardcover edition as follows:
Fraser, Steve, 1945–
Wall Street : America's dream palace / Steve Fraser.
p. cm.—(Icons of America series)
Includes bibliographical references and index.
ISBN 978-0-300-11755-4 (alk. paper)
1. Capitalists and financiers—United States—Biography.   2. Wall Street (New York, N.Y.)—History.   I. Title.
HG172.A2F72 2008
332.64'273—dc22   2007035453

ISBN 978-0-300-15143-5 (pbk.)

A catalogue record for this book is available from the British Library.

10 9 8 7 6 5 4 3 2 1

Illustration credits: p. viii: *New York Stock Exchange* © 2007 Jupiterimages Corporation; p. 10: *KING* © Art Parts; p. 54: *SHAKDOWN* © Art Parts; p. 96: *WOW_019* © Image Club/Getty Images; p. 134: *EXEC_DVL* © Art Parts; p. 174: *EASY_MNY* © Art Parts

Icons of America
Mark Crispin Miller, Series Editor

Icons of America is a series of short works by leading scholars, critics, and
writers on American history, or more properly the image of America
in American history, through the lens of a single iconic individual,
event, object, or cultural phenomenon. Other titles in the series include:

Alger Hiss and the Battle for History, by Susan Jacoby
Frankly, My Dear: Gone with the Wind *Revisited*,
by Molly Haskell
Fred Astaire, by Joseph Epstein
Gypsy: The Art of the Tease, by Rachel Shteir
The Hamburger: A History, by Josh Ozersky
Inventing a Nation: Washington, Adams, Jefferson, by Gore Vidal
King's Dream, by Eric J. Sundquist
*Nearest Thing to Heaven: The Empire State Building and
American Dreams*, by Mark Kingwell
Small Wonder: The Little Red Schoolhouse in History and Memory,
by Jonathan Zimmerman

Forthcoming titles include:
Arthur C. Danto on Andy Warhol
Toni Bentley on George Balanchine
Stephen Cox on "The Big House"
Tom DeHaven on Superman

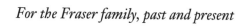

For the Fraser family, past and present

Contents

Introduction 1

ONE
The Aristocrat 11

TWO
The Confidence Man 55

THREE
The Hero 97

FOUR
The Immoralist 135

Epilogue 175
Notes 181
Acknowledgments 193
Index 195

NEW YORK STOCK EXCHANGE.

Introduction

It seems like a dream to me.
DANIEL DREW

Wall Street. No other place on earth is so singularly identified with money and the power of money. Wall Street is not a street; it is "the Street." To invoke its name is to conjure up capitalism in all its imperial grandeur. It stands as an unbreachable bulwark defending a commercial order that began when the nation was born. The Street gives off an incandescent glow fired not simply by wealth but by wealth burnished with a patina of prudential sobriety and social preeminence. Deliberation and caution mark its weighty proceedings. Inside its monumental piles of granite, steel, and glass, the equations of economic fitness are calculated with mathematical rigor. Like its very name—the street of streets—it exudes a certain quintessential purity. It hovers above and at some remove from the messiness of the workaday world, distilling its numerical truth, compelling obedience to a

I

higher rationality. Admired or reviled, Wall Street is the towering symbol of a cool, impregnable power.

Yet Wall Street also evokes a radically different set of symbolic
associations as the center of mad ambition. Fevers, manias, and
frenzies race up and down its pavement like hysterics in a lunatic
asylum. Life on the Street cycles between irrational ecstasies and
depressive panics. This is the land of financial "wilding." Here one
indulges all dreams. Here one gambles recklessly on the future.
No one is denied entrance to this democracy of the greedy. No one
need kowtow to the established order. Irreverence is revered. The
world is created anew each day. Wall Street is a carnival, the world
turned upside down, where today's confidence man is tomorrow's
financial seer, a boulevard of endless opportunity and endemic disaster. A hot zone of credulous fools and knowing gamesmen, the
Street defies the very orderliness, discipline, and self-abnegating
labor of the capitalism it presumably embodies and symbolizes. It
rises up in the imagination as an urban demimonde, notorious
for its facile swindlers and lupine parasites, where the illicit dream
of effortless wealth corrupts and disorders all it touches.

Lodged deep within our collective psyche these contending
incongruent images of Wall Street illuminate its paradoxical history in American culture, suggesting that Main Street and Wall
Street have found themselves in a strange love-hate codepen-
dency for a very long time.

In a culture preoccupied with questions of sin and salvation,
Wall Street has served as a protean metaphor. At various times

and places, it has stood in for the rich, big business, the "money power," parvenu greed, financial piracy, high society on parade, moral and sexual prostitution, Jewish or Anglo-Saxon or capitalist conspiracy, Yankee parasitism, the American Century, the land of Aladdin, and a good deal more. Its truths have been multiple and self-contradictory: deviant and legitimate; heroic and villainous; aristocratic and plebian; rational and insane; anarchic and orderly; liberating and oppressive; muscular and unmanly; libidinal and inhibited; corporate and freebooting; patriotic and treasonous; indispensable and profligate. A vital part of our national iconography, Wall Street has drawn its energy from the antipodes of our moral, social, and intellectual obsessions.

So it is that through the years Wall Street has inspired dreams and nightmares deep inside American culture, leaving its imprint on the lives of ordinary as well some extraordinary people. These private reveries and collective fantasies tell us something fundamental about the Street and its intensely charged role in the national saga. And they do more than that: they tell us something about the mind of Wall Street, but also something about the Wall Streets of the American mind.

Four apparitions especially have captured the popular imagination: the aristocrat, the confidence man, the hero, and the immoralist. These images, while hardly exhausting Wall Street's metaphorical mother lode, have proven the most durable and capacious. As an ensemble they encompass the whole history of the Street, beginning with the American Revolution and running through our own vexed relationship with "the Street of dreams" at the turn of the new millennium. *Wall Street* takes a look at these four faces of Wall Street: where they came from, how they have changed along with the country, and why they have proved so enduring.

Wall Street has long nourished its reputation as a hothouse of aristocratic, un-American hauteur. Antipathy toward aristocracy was always a primal element of the national credo. But if ever there was a natural habitat for the nurturing of such an alien species, Wall Street seemed to many to be that place. Aristocratic associations shadowed the Street from the beginning. Condemned first by Thomas Jefferson as counterrevolutionary "tories," denizens of the Street were still being ostracized by FDR a century and half later as "economic royalists." During the imperial age of J. P. Morgan, opposition fixated on Wall Street's frightening omnipotence; after the Great Crash of 1929, however, it was instead the Street's omni-incompetence that made it seem a contemptible as well as a despised and illegitimate aristocratic elite. Indeed, the obloquy that blanketed Wall Street like a funeral shroud consigned it to cultural exile for a long generation, silencing its metaphorical resonance in the public imagination until the age of Reagan.

If the aristocrat seemed a noxious import from the Old World, the confidence man was a native son, born and raised within the American grain. He frequented a different Wall Street, a zone of libidinal desire, a seductive underground peopled by the "penniless plutocrat" and the "dream millionaire." Flourishing first during the Jacksonian era, confidence men shared the "dream" of instant wealth with their credulous victims. This was Abraham Lincoln's land of democratic opportunity minus all the hard work, the parsimony, the slow, laborious rise through the ranks of dependent labor into the liberated air of propertied independence. Here desires and forms of behavior that otherwise violated the norms of respectable middle-class morality were licensed, even celebrated. Wall Street confidence men thrived especially whenever the economy boomed, gulling low and high alike: former President Grant in the 1880s; anonymous masses following after Charles Ponzi during the Roaring Twenties; addictive day-traders afloat on the dot.com bubble of the 1990s. The confidence man manipulated the covetous impulses of his marks, encouraging an irreverent disregard for the maxims of self-renunciatory work and provision for the future. He offered a dream capitalism, weightless, without the gravity of production to hold it down. In those innocent antebellum years unlettered youths from small towns and farms in the American hinterland, relying on their own wits, audacity, and rubbery ethics, could imagine standing toe to toe with baronial financiers and coming out on top. So too more than century later, during the age of what one writer called "the dot.con," men from nowhere, without social pedigrees or Ivy League educations, would dream of unhorsing Wall Street's "white shoe" aristocrats, along the way gulling a whole nation to buy into their improbable fantasies.

Sometimes these confidence men underwent a marvelous transformation and became the colossi they adulated, emerging as another Wall Street icon, the hero. The names of Cornelius Vanderbilt ("the Commodore"), "Jubilee Jim" (also known as "the Admiral") Fisk, and Jay ("the Mephistopheles of Wall Street") Gould are legendary, the first generation of Wall Street conquistadors. Often from unprepossessing backgrounds, unsavory—shady even—they soon entered the national consciousness as Napoleonic heroes, in part because these men from nowhere seemed to affirm the most grandiose versions of the American dream. Others would follow. Some, like J. P. Morgan, hailed from the blue-blooded ranks of America's upper class. No matter what their origins they shared a striking profile. The Wall Street hero was an empire builder: a conqueror of Mother Nature, of the marketplace, of other men, of himself. He lived his life as an ongoing encounter with chance, the hot breath of disaster at his back. These titans never blinked. They stayed cool when lesser men panicked. When the situation demanded it they could be intemperate, irreverent, and implacable. The Wall Street hero embodied a distinctive style of masculine prowess. The dramaturgy of the Street, beginning with the founding generation of "robber barons," has always borrowed heavily from languages of warrior cultures: cowboy colloquialisms as well as Greek and medieval mythology. Gunslingers and mighty hunters, titans and gorgons, barons and white knights have stalked Wall Street's imaginary canyons from the prehensile days of Fisk and Vanderbilt to the cybernetic sleekness of Michael Milken, inhabiting a world brimming over with animal virility and vitality.

Even the Wall Street hero, however—not to mention the aris-

Introduction

tocrat and the confidence man—has aroused the deepest popular suspicions. Americans were appalled by the same men they admired. Wall Street seemed to breed sinners, moral as well as social decadents, as it filled up with people who accumulated wealth without effort. For a society profoundly, if sometimes also sanctimoniously, committed to the work ethic and the dignity of labor, this was worrying evidence of a debilitating canker eating away at the moral fiber of the republic. After all, what Wall Street did struck most Americans as a mysterious (and secretive and dangerous) form of gambling, itself widely treated as a fatal sin by nineteenth-century American Protestantism. Worse than that, the Street ran a crooked game, which favored a privileged circle of insiders. And worse still, Wall Street amassed its fabulous riches like a parasite, living off the fruits of the honest labor of impoverished farmers, sweated industrial workers, and self-sacrificing, frugal entrepreneurs. The Wall Street sinner occupied a kind of moral gulag, a place where cupidity, which otherwise ran rampant in a society given over to material acquisitiveness, could be isolated, condemned, and exiled to psychological safety. The Wall Street operator, given over to delusional speculation and addictive gambling, disdainful of work, and, if rich enough, parading his dandified manners in absurdly pretentious getups at gilded soirees, was a perfect scapegoat for a culture steeped in Protestant guilt yet overrun with material cravings. The visage of the Wall Street immoralist darkened the horizon of the Gilded Age, still haunted the American imagination a half century later

7

during the Great Depression, and reappeared as Gordon Gekko, the notorious cinematic invoker of "Greed is good."

All these Wall Street figures of the American mind—the pretentious aristocrat, the wily confidence man, the imperial hero, the soulless sinner—lived at some social as well as psychic remove from the people. By and large, until recently Wall Street was a rather exclusive domain, a realm millions gazed at in wonderment or revulsion but rarely imagined as their own. Much has changed during our own time. The "democratizing" of the Street happened with lightning speed during the past half century. Suddenly Everyman was invited to feel at home there. The triumph of free-market thinking prepared the way. So too did the "Wall Street 'R' Us" mentality first assiduously cultivated back in the 1950s by "bullish on America" Charles Merrill, the founder of Merrill Lynch. The deindustrialization of America during the last quarter of the twentieth century diminished the cultural gravity of "productive labor," once a hallowed element of the national credo. For great numbers of ordinary people—at least until the dot.com bubble burst—the market had become a "living entity—ticking away at the breakfast table, at the gym, at the office." City streets lit up like a twenty-four-hour-a-day theater of numbers, tracking the rhythms of the global stock market on billboards, eye-level flat screens, and rotating digital cryptographs: a universal spectacle and nonstop economic EKG.

Wall Street's recent ascension in the popular mind suggests, among other things, that the old taboos have withered—the ones that sanctioned hard work as a covenant with God and community. This happened once before during the Jazz Age, when a zanily inflated stock market, together with bootleg gin and the flapper, signaled the brief advent of a culture of sensual release. The Great Depression put a crushing stop to that. Yet those illicit, subterranean desires were always one secret of Wall Street's allure. When Wall Street rose up again during the Reagan era, they flourished uninhibited. But so too did all the old mythic images of the Street. Today's crony capitalists can't help but remind us of those Gilded Age financial aristocrats whose power was so great it threatened to undermine the basic institutions of democratic government. Enron and the cascade of financial scandals that followed in its wake recall with a shudder an age-old fear of the confidence man. During his halcyon days Michael Milken seemed to perform the same economic heroics that made J. P. Morgan into an admired colossus. And the unabashed greediness of Carl Icahn made it clear that the Wall Street immoralist was alive and well.

Each of the Street's four faces shares features with his mythic brethren: the aristocrat is a sinner, the sinner a confidence man, the hero is a man of the people but also an elitist. For just this reason, Wall Street stands at the metaphorical heart of American capitalism. As we enter America's Dream Palace, then, we are confronted by an enigma: How has it been possible for the Street to absorb the honorific codes and metaphors of the warrior culture while living under the ignoble sign of the parasite? How can it be that the same avenue has come to stand for elite economic and political domination even as it functions as a dreamscape of plebian ambition?

ONE

The Aristocrat

William Duer was running for his life. An enraged mob was chasing him through the streets of New York. If they caught up with him they would beat him to a pulp . . . or worse. Luckily for Duer the sheriff got there first. While his pursuers cried, "We will have Mr. Duer, he has gotten our money," he was hauled off to jail, where he would spend his few remaining years. Once a man of distinction and wealth, William Duer was now ruined, left to contemplate what might have been.[1]

The year was 1792, and Wall Street had just experienced its first crash, for which William Duer and a secret circle of New York grandees were mainly to blame. They had conspired to speculate on the bonds just issued by the newly created federal government. Soon they found themselves deeply overcommitted and forced to liquidate their holdings, causing the fledgling market to collapse and its manipulators to flee—in Duer's case to debtors' prison; for the more fortunate among them to safer havens out of state. Even though there was no formal or even informal stock exchange in those days; even though the local economy went about its business largely unaffected by the mysterious machinations of financiers, there were still plenty of ordinary people who suffered. Real estate prices collapsed, credit dried up, house building stopped. The general distress spread from businessmen to "shopkeepers, Widows, orphans, Butchers, Cartmen, Gardeners, market women and even the noted Bawd, Mrs. McCarty."[2]

What made Mrs. McCarty and her neighbors irate was something more than their own losses, grievous as these might be. They and many of their fellow citizens hated Duer and his confederates not only for what they'd done but for who they were. The Revolution had just ended, and tempers had barely cooled. Suspicions and animosities directed against covert monarchists and Tory aristocrats still electrified the political atmosphere. And Wall Street's first inside traders seemed to match that ignominious profile.

After all, William Duer was a merchant prince. He lived in manorial splendor on a Hudson River estate, catered to by liveried servants—this at a moment when dressing the help in livery was considered a deliberate provocation aimed at the democratic sentiments of American patriots. A onetime officer in the British army, educated at Eton, Duer was the offspring of a wealthy West Indian planter. He had migrated to colonial New York in hope of enhancing his fortune. Once there he had married into the highest echelons of colonial society. His wife, "Lady Kitty," was the second daughter of General William Alexander, who laid claim to a Scottish earldom. Lady Kitty's grandfather was Philip Livingston, a prominent member of New York's most distinguished family dynasty. Duer's closest friends and associates included other great dynastic clans of old Dutch New York: the Macombs and the Roosevelts, among others. His commercial interests extended from powder-, saw-, and gristmills to distilleries and maritime supplies.

While Duer had supported the Revolution (indeed, he was a member of the Continental Congress and a signatory of the Articles of Confederation), he was widely suspected of profiteering at its expense. He sold, at inflated prices, precious supplies of timber and planks for barracks and ships to Washington's desperate army of independence. He provisioned the Continental Army with horses, ammunition, cattle, and feed but was suspected of hoarding supplies of rum and blankets, and even of engaging in sub-rosa trading with the enemy. After the Revolution, Duer escalated his pursuit of social elevation and material enrichment, a quest that culminated in his fateful attempt to corner the market in government securities. And here he was counting on a special bit of good fortune: he was a confidant of the nation's first secretary of the treasury, Alexander Hamilton.[3]

Hamilton was a Revolutionary War hero and a founding father. But by the 1790s, he was also the man most widely suspected of harboring elitist sentiments dangerous to the democratic aspirations of the new nation. During the Constitutional debates he had argued on behalf of a lifetime presidency and imagined the Senate as a kind of House of Lords. In his capacity as President George Washington's secretary of the treasury, he had devised a plan for funding the national debt that had accumulated during the war and in the years afterward. The federal government would sell its own bonds to make good on the nearly worthless securities issued by the states and the Continental Congress during the Revolution. Hamilton assumed that the purchasers of these new securities would be merchants, bankers, and others of substantial means. By acquiring these bonds they would help establish the creditworthiness of the new nation. In turn, that would, Hamilton hypothesized, attract capital from home and abroad which would jump-start the commercial and industrial development of what was, after all, an underdeveloped country.

Hamilton was candid in his view that the new government ought to rely on men of social eminence and wealth. Their resources and public-mindedness made them uniquely prepared to lead the nation, or so he thought. They would constitute a vanguard whose financial wherewithal and disinterested commitment to the nation's welfare would help realize his vision of America's one day joining the ranks of the world's great powers. Hamilton himself came from inauspicious social beginnings, a West Indian of illegitimate birth. But he felt an affinity for New York's patricians, having married Elizabeth Schuyler, the daughter of General Philip Schuyler, war hero and patriarch of a venerable

Knickerbocker clan, one of the Hudson River patroons. Hamilton trusted these circles implicitly, convinced of their rectitude and devotion to the country's future fame and glory. He was infatuated with caste and riches. The problem was that people like Duer turned out to be less public-spirited than Hamilton supposed.[4]

Duer's ties to the Schuyler clan afforded him access to Hamilton, who appointed him an assistant secretary of the treasury. Duer and his "6 percent club" of fellow speculators hoped for inside information on the government's pricing of its new securities in order to get a jump on the market. Hamilton, whose integrity was irreproachable, rebuffed Duer and warned him against gambling on the national debt. Duer, ignoring him, crashed and burned, as would many a Wall Street inside trader over the next two centuries. Much of Duer's estate was liquidated at sheriff's sale. Lady Kitty lived out her life in severely straitened circumstances, dwelling at the edge of fashionable society and compelled to take in genteel boarders. Moreover, as the struggle between the followers of Hamilton and Jefferson over the fate of the American Revolution grew ever nastier during the 1790s, Hamilton's rumored connection to the Duer plot kept resurfacing.[5]

Indeed, in 1797 Hamilton felt compelled to publicly acknowledge an adulterous affair with the wife of a Duer accomplice while passionately denying that he had ever conspired to enrich himself or others at the nation's expense. He denounced his "Jacobin" enemies—Jefferson and James Madison especially—accusing them of pandering to the prejudices of the mob and slandering his reputation in order to subvert his efforts to turn America into a great commercial republic. And he was not entirely wrong.[6]

Jefferson, Madison, and other leading Democratic-Republicans had known of the treasury secretary's sexual transgressions for years but never seriously suspected him of public corruption. However, they were vehemently opposed to Hamilton's financial and mercantile plans: to his proposals to create a national debt, establish a national bank, and subsidize manufacturing in the infant nation. Jefferson and his allies were not against trade. But they envisioned an agrarian republic, not a commercial one, made up of independent middling farmers trading with Europe only for those necessities not produced at home. In this way the new nation would be immunized against the infection of urban luxury and squalor, the war of class against class, and the moral rot that they felt characterized the Old World. Those mysterious arteries of finance, in particular, were the portals through which this political disease could most easily penetrate the healthy social organism.

Nor was the danger strictly economic or moral. Hamilton's "Jacobin" enemies were not merely opposed to his plans; they saw them as part of a malevolent conspiracy to build up a "moneyed aristocracy" allied to the government which would inevitably undermine the democratic accomplishments of the Revolution. Duer was viewed as a felonious member of this anti-republican "aristocratic faction." In a word, Hamilton's alleged connection to his Wall Street confreres embodied, in miniature, the Tory Counterrevolution.

As the Democratic-Republicans saw it, this was a plot to establish a financial aristocracy like the one ensconced in England. Looking across the ocean they could easily see how an incestuous relationship between the money men and the central government (in England, the monarchy; in America, presumably, the executive branch) threatened to make the government the exclusive preserve of the privileged. The great executive powers of France and Great Britain, so the anti-monarchists believed, floated on a vast sea of public debt. That funded debt had in turn engendered big banking institutions, well-oiled markets for money, new forms of investment, and a whole new class that traded in public securities. An alliance between this moneyed class and the Crown had overawed independent sources of political authority. According to Jefferson the real sin in Hamilton's design was that it would "prepare the way for a change from the present republican form of government to that of a monarchy of which the English constitution is to be the model." This was perhaps the inevitable fate of the Old World, but it was precisely to avoid this fate in the New that people had fought and died. Wall Street thus found itself on the front lines of a war between aristocracy and democracy. With stakes that high, exploiting the enemy's sexual peccadilloes seemed an excusable political tactic.[7]

Partisans of Jefferson tirelessly spread the alarm. All through the 1790s, publicists, pamphleteers, and politicians warned about bankers and speculators fattening on the public credit. Even President Washington, who in the end favored Hamilton's strategy, worried, and he queried the treasury secretary: Would not the new capital ultimately pose a threat to republican government by "a corrupt squadron of paper dealers"? Hamilton's plan was a bonanza for such people, an unholy alliance of aristocracy and money. These speculators had bought up the securities issued by the states and the Continental Congress at rock-bottom prices from their original holders: desperate veterans, farmers, and other ordinary folk. Under Hamilton's scheme these rich bond buyers could now redeem their once worthless paper at its full face value.[8]

War was waged in churches and by sensationalist pamphleteers; in novels, poems, and newspaper doggerel; on the stage in theatrical satires; and in furious political jeremiads. In his satiric "Chronology of Facts" in the *National Gazette*, Philip Freneau pronounced 1791 the "Reign of the Speculators." He invented a mock plan for the creation of an American aristocracy whose meticulously graded and serried ranks mirrored rising levels of speculative practice from "the lower order of the Leech" to the middling "Their Huckstership" on to the sublime "Order of the Scrip." Jefferson inveighed against the sleaziness and injustice practiced by those who bought up worthless "continentals": "Speculators had made a trade of cozening them from their holders. . . . Couriers and relay horses by land, and swift sailing pilot boats by sea, were flying in all directions," buying up paper securities so that "immense sums were thus filched from the poor and ignorant." Madison worried that "the stock-jobbers will become the praetorian band of the Government, at once its tool and its

tyrant; bribed by its largesse, and overawing it by clamorous combinations." John Adams, who often allied himself with Hamilton
and shared with the treasury secretary a conservative conviction
about the inevitability of social class distinctions, nonetheless
observed that "paper wealth has been the source of aristocracy in
this country, as well as landed wealth, with a vengeance."[9]

When Duer's speculative bubble burst popular revulsion was
palpable. Speculators became derisively known as "Hamilton's
Rangers" and "Paper Hunters." Newssheets filled with talk of
"scriptomania," "scripponomy," and "scriptophobia." A Phila-
delphian, writing to his local newspaper, anguished over his efforts
to find safe passage through the factional battlefield. Although
loath to join the local Jeffersonian Democratic Society, he still
wanted to reassure his neighbors that he was certainly "no tory,
no British agent, no speculator." Madison summed up the moral
and political outrage: "There must be something wrong, radically
and morally and politically wrong, in a system which transfers
the reward from those who paid the most valuable of all considerations, to those who scarcely paid any consideration at all."[10]

There is a grand irony at the core of this political dramaturgy,
an irony that would infuse American attitudes about Wall Street
for generations to come. Both sides of this fateful confrontation
were right, yet both chased after phantoms. Hamilton had envisioned enlightened men investing for the public good. Jefferson
saw "sharpers" and "gambling scoundrels." Both turned out to
be correct, as the sad career of William Duer, an enlightened

scoundrel if ever there was one, exemplified. But both founding fathers were at the same time wrong as they prophesied a final conflict between enemies that were more imaginary than real.

Hamilton was hardly a feudal aristocrat. Nor did he harbor serious thoughts of resurrecting a titled aristocracy in the New World. He did, however, entertain real anxieties about "mobocracy" and genuinely feared the leveling instincts of the "Jacobin" democracy, which seemed to him ready to countenance the wholesale repudiation of lawful contractual obligations. But the respectable freeholders of town and country were hardly revolutionary levelers. There were no bloodthirsty sansculottes preparing to erect guillotines; nor were farmers, however angry about government excise taxes and other matters—as Shays's Rebellion suggested—ready to burn down the manorial estates of their feudal overlords in some version of an American jacquerie. Moreover, alongside this fanciful specter Hamilton cultivated a parallel consoling delusion that men like Duer (if not Duer himself) were capable of a kind of disinterested behavior that is sometimes associated with an idealized version of the virtuous aristocrat. Funding the national debt would help nurture a national ruling class, a regime of "the wise, the rich, and the good." He was convinced that "those who are most commonly creditors of the nation, are generally speaking, enlightened men." He said of the rich and well born: "Their vices are probably more favorable to the prosperity of the State than those of the indigent and partake less of moral depravity." But it turned out, to Hamilton's chagrin, that modern commercial society—the kind of society he championed for America—bred men of commerce whose commitment to public service often took a distant back seat to the pursuit of the main chance. That was Hamilton's dilemma, one William Duer exemplified.[11]

So too, the Jeffersonian democrats attacked what they thought of as an aristocracy. But it turned out to be a fledgling plutocracy. True enough, this capitalist-minded untitled elite would now and again try to assume the trappings of the pedigreed aristocracy, if only to beef up its presumptive right to rule and its own social self-confidence. In New York, the Federalist followers of Hamilton formed the Knights of the Dagger to assault Democratic-Republicans, dispersing their public rallies and tearing down their Liberty Poles. William Duer's son was one such Knight. Dressing like aristocrats, decorating their homes, horses, and carriages with heraldic crests, cultivating the accents of the British upper class, hosting fancy-dress balls and fetes, and otherwise aping the customs and mores of European gentility were very much in vogue among the Federalists of Hamilton's day, as they would be again, more emphatically, during the Gilded Age at the turn of the twentieth century. John Pintard, one of Duer's co-conspirators who only escaped debtors' prison by fleeing New York, was at the same time a man of distinctive cultural refinement, a founder of the New-York Historical Society, an author of works on medicine and topography, and an expert on Indian cultures. (He later returned to New York and resumed a lucrative career on the

Street.) Without question many a Federalist openly admired the English constitution, especially the way it institutionalized social hierarchy. Federalists scarcely concealed their hopes—their expectations, actually—that a similarly deferential political order would install itself in America and that they would preside over it. Secretary of State John Jay, Hamilton's good friend and political ally, candidly asserted that "those who own the country ought to govern it."[12]

In the end, however, William Duer's insatiable acquisitiveness gave the game away. He and his cohorts viewed the new nation as an incomparable opportunity to indulge in the pursuit of happiness. For them, as for so many of their fellow citizens, this meant the pursuit of property. But it was precisely that fellowship of desire uniting the aristocrat with the commoner that comprised the Jeffersonian side of the dilemma. Smallholding farmers, artisans, and shopkeepers, the living body of the Jeffersonian anti-aristocratic persuasion, were themselves wholly invested in the same quest for propertied independence, albeit on a more modest scale. Time and again in the years that followed, struggling farmers, anti-monopoly small businessmen, upstart entrepreneurs in search of start-up capital, railroad workers, coal miners, artisans, and laborers suffering under industrial tyranny would single out Wall Street as their archenemy. Just as commonly, however, they would depict those rapacious financiers as if they were not so much a capitalist plutocracy as a blue-blooded aristocracy, an alien species, running against the American grain.

This conflation of capitalist with aristocrat would define one iconic image of Wall Street for a century and more. It reflected on the one hand a traditional strain in American political culture that began with the Revolution. It was as well an evasion, also typically American: a way to avoid condemning capitalism outright (when in fact so many shared a dream of some future democratic version of capitalism) while still venting enormous rage at the inequalities and exploitation that trailed in the wake of capitalist development. Duer's panic and the ferocious name-calling between Hamiltonian Federalists and Jeffersonian Republicans signaled an underlying ambivalence about the import of an incipient commercial civilization. Wall Street seemed to epitomize that ambivalence. Was it pimping for monarchy or incubating the glorious birth of a rich and powerful republic? Was it a cockpit of counterrevolution or a modern engine of revolutionary progress?

Moreover, this ambivalence was aided and abetted by the extravagant aristocratic arrogance and supercilious playacting of the country's burgeoning class of financial-industrial nouveaux riches. Never would this melding of aristocrat and plutocrat leave a more indelible imprint on Wall Street than during the heyday of America's Industrial Revolution, its Gilded Age.

■

Fear of counterrevolution shadowed American politics for well over a century. This may strike us as surprising. Nowadays we are accustomed to thinking about the national saga as the uninterrupted procession of democracy, first into the ranks of white males and then to former slaves, women, minorities, and others once excluded from its privileges. But millions of citizens confronted by the earth-shattering economic and social turmoil of America's Industrial Revolution were filled with foreboding about the rise of an oligarchy so powerful it seemed bent on subverting and seizing control of all the institutions of democratic government. No one doubted that the conspiracy had its headquarters on Wall Street. After all, by the late nineteenth century the Street had invaded all the main arteries of the economy, its railroads and new industrial corporations as well as the lines of credit that kept American farmers in business.

Except for Lincoln's victory in 1860, no presidential election of the nineteenth century aroused as much passion or the same ominous sense that the country's fate hung in the balance as did the confrontation between William Jennings Bryan and William H. McKinley in 1896. When the "Boy Orator of the Platte" memorably vowed that he and the Democratic Party would not allow mankind to be crucified on a cross of gold, Wall Street shuddered. Every dispossessed farmer and every small businessman sinking beneath a sea of debt knew instinctively just who and what Bryan was referring to. For two decades and more the Street had earned the enmity of all those who sought economic salvation through some form of debt relief. Mainly they demanded the untethering of the nation from the gold standard and proposed to inflate the currency by coining silver or issuing greenbacks. Dominant business interests, especially the leading New York banks, staunchly resisted, warning that such a sacrilege would lead straight to economic bedlam. By the time of the 1896 election the country was suffering through the third year of a depression more cataclysmic than anyone could remember. The temperature of political life had reached the boiling point.

While most metropolitan dailies endorsed McKinley, the New York editor Joseph Pulitzer opened his pages to the opposition. A month before the election, he turned over the Sunday magazine supplement of his *New York World* to Tom Watson, the firebrand populist governor of Georgia and vice presidential candidate of the People's Party. Watson had just visited Wall Street, and his article, "Wall Street Conspiracies Against the American Nation," skewered the Street as an incubator of aristocratic counterrevolution. An accompanying cartoon featured a giant snake rising out of its nesting place in the Stock Exchange to strangle the businessman, the farmer, and the worker. "A name more thoroughly detested is not to be found in the vocabulary of American politics"—Wall Street, in Watson's eyes, was a breeding ground for depression, empty houses, and barren fields. It was a hideout for conspirators who in turn controlled President Grover Cleveland and his cabinet. Indeed, "since our Republic was founded no president has been so bland and sterile a Wall Street tool." The corruptor of legislatures, the bench, the press, and the ballot box itself, "Here is Wall Street: we see the actual rulers of the Republic. They are kings. . . . The Government itself lies prone in the dust with the iron heel of Wall Street upon its neck." Watson was no advocate of violent revolution; he placed what remained of his hope in the vote. Nor did he fear, as did sizable numbers of upper-class Americans, a "revolution rising among the poor. The revolution I fear is coming from Wall Street." If victorious it would crush the spirit and achievement of 1776, a tragic denouement to Jefferson's prophetic warnings about a moneyed aristocracy.[13]

Watson's ire was felt by millions. And it was stoked not only by Wall Street's apparent political usurpations but also by its social provocations. Mark Twain and Charles Dudley Warner anointed the moment America's "Gilded Age" in their best-selling novel of the same title, a hilarious send-up of the era's mercenary mania and political bombast. Many other social observers were struck by the vulgarity, vainglory, and appalling social insensitivity of what today we would call "the rich and famous." Members of America's upper classes, many of them newly risen out of social obscurity and not so sure themselves of what justified their sudden preeminence, staged a great vanity fair, outdoing one another in ostentatious displays of their truly enormous wealth. With some hyperbole a contemporary observer noted, "The entire population of the country entered the field. . . . Broadway was lined with carriages. The fashionable milliners, dress-makers, and jewelers reaped golden harvests. The pageant of Fifth Avenue on Sunday and of Central Park during the week-days was bizarre, gorgeous, wonderful! Never were such dinners, such receptions, such balls. . . . Vanity Fair was no longer a dream."[14]

All of this luxury could arouse feelings of revulsion. *Harper's New Monthly* scathingly noted that a single act of gluttony at Delmonico's or La Maison Dorée could support a soldier and his family for much of a year. If people had managed to gratify their greediest appetites even during the Civil War, then the outbreak of peace relaxed all remaining restraints. The lavishness of the social scene bordered on the grotesque. Mrs. Hamilton Fish hosted a party for her friends' dogs in which the "guests" were presented with diamond necklace party favors and a place of honor at the table was reserved for an ape. The financier Leonard Jerome erected a palace on Madison Avenue equipped with a theater to seat six hundred and carpeted stables paneled in black walnut. The "flash age" had arrived, its gaudy show presided over by August Belmont of the Rothschild bank and his Wall Street cronies.[15]

Wealth alone, however, was not enough to shore up a shaky sense of entitlement. America's nouveaux riches, so many of whose overnight great fortunes derived from Wall Street, made up for their lack of familial lineage, social breeding, and cultural bona fides by pretending to be an aristocracy. Ensconced in fortress-like urban mansions and country villas, decked out in the latest continental fashions (British for the men, French for the women), riding about in thoroughbred-driven equipages bearing counterfeit coats-of-arms, ministered to by liveried servants, hunting to hounds, gathering at costume balls festooned with exotic orchids and jeweled party favors where they feasted on nightingale tongues and rare forms of animal and vegetable life, America's social elite erected an elaborate and deliberately visible feudal fantasy world. That the country's upper classes went around masquerading as Henry VIII, Louis XIV, and Marie Antoinette; confecting aristocratic genealogies; marrying off their daughters (dubbed "dollar princesses" by mesmerized journalists) to bankrupt, frequently dissolute, but titled Europeans; transplanting castles, stone by stone, from the French countryside to Fifth Avenue; and buying up a millennium's worth of high art from a half dozen civilizations and setting it all down helter-skelter in drafty auditorium-sized living rooms may strike us as farcical. And certainly such theatrics expressed their own transparent social and cultural insecurity, an attempt to find a toehold in a remarkably vertiginous society. But this social masquerade could also be galling beyond endurance.

Wall Street's flirtation with aristocracy had changed fundamentally since Hamilton's day. Beneath this veneer of heraldic pomp and clubby exclusivity something irreducibly fake showed through, leaving these nouveaux riches ripe for ridicule. An artist's rendering of "one of the Upper Ten Thousand" sketched a risible image of a strutting, pouting, pompous, top-hatted New York swell. After all, it was an American birthright to distrust and unmask aristocracy. This rising elite was not only privileged, like the old one, not only arrogant, like the old one, but carried with

it as well newer attributes of financial jobbery and reckless speculation that were peculiarly associated with a Wall Street that had
become in the eyes of one reformer, "a Street of Palaces." Referred to over and over again as a "shoddy aristocracy"—the in-
tent was to compare these parvenus to the cheap fabric made from
reclaimed wool—it was a class whose bona fides were forever
under scrutiny. Even a Wall Street insider like William Fowler
found himself appalled, writing an exposé of the typical denizen
of the Street, dressed in purple and fine linen, gorging on delica-
cies and "wines of the vintage of Waterloo," drinking out of cut
Bohemian glass; a creature who "produces nothing, . . . drives no
plough, plies no hammer, sends no shuttle flashing through the
loom."[16]

Families like the Duers and the Rennselaers were both more
credible and less powerful than pretend aristocrats like the Vanderbilts and the Goulds. Back then Wall Street still moved to the
stately rhythms of the gentlemen's club, trading with prudential
deliberation small quantities of government bonds and the im-
peccably safe securities of dowagers. Its influence on the surrounding economy was measurable but not decisive. The men
who worked there may have lacked medieval family pedigrees,
but they were classically educated, managed their landed estates
while dabbling in financial affairs, were bred to assume positions
of social leadership, and lived amid a political culture where it
was still the custom to defer to one's "natural" betters.

Much of that world had vaporized in the industrial and financial revolution that followed the Civil War. Wall Street had become a zone of frenzied speculation, of monomaniacal exaltation and panic: a hypnotic spectacle of moneymaking and money losing watched by millions. Many of the men who drove the country's economic revolution from Wall Street—people like Cornelius Vanderbilt, Daniel Drew, Jim Fisk, Russell Sage, and Jay Gould—were instant millionaires who could make no plausible claim to social or political entitlement, unlike their Federalist era forebears. Even if they tried to, which they sometimes did, they were usually unsuccessful: Americans had long ago jettisoned their earlier habits of political deference. Indeed, as the hierarchies of wealth and income grew ever steeper in the late nineteenth century, the democratic sentiments of the populace only grew stronger. Political life in the United States, at least on the surface, was emphatically anti-elitist, run by urban machines and professional politicians who made it their business to cater to the egalitarian instincts of their constituents.

But the sheer economic throw weight of the new Wall Street was immeasurably greater than anything the old Federalist gentry had exercised or even imagined. The Street ran (and occasionally mismanaged or deliberately looted) the national railroad network, the country's single most important industry and the strategic heart of its infrastructure. More than that, Wall Street housed the engine room which transformed the structure of industry, providing the capital resources and organizational inventiveness that gave birth to the modern, publicly traded corporation and thereby to the modern economy. United States Steel, General Electric, and International Harvester were but a few of the household names of American business midwifed and often controlled by the Street's great investment banks. It was on the Street that the nation's great undertakings—its coast-to-coast railroads and stupendous agricultural output; its gigantic steel, oil, and raw materials industries; its pioneering technologies in electricity and chemicals—were alchemized. It was there that all the critical capital transactions originated, where the shrewdest political advice was available, where new insights into cost accounting were devised and revised. Here New York's investment bankers and brokers turned the tangible wherewithal of the country into its paper facsimile, a virtual economy whose very liquidity made possible the mobilizing of ever greater capital funds to further enlarge the scope, efficiency, and power of the whole U.S. economy.

A select circle of great New York banks—the House of Morgan first of all, but also Kuhn, Loeb; Harriman Brothers; Dillon Read; Brown Brothers; the Belmont-Rothschild interests—were themselves linked to a network of other financial institutions (insurance companies, investment trusts, commercial banks). Consequently, they occupied a commanding position over much of the country's reservoir of liquid capital. Access to that pool was a matter of life and death for modern industrial enterprises increasingly dependent on larger and more technically complex units of production. Wall Street became the new economy's gatekeeper. It could to some substantial degree determine what, how, and where business thrived or died, whether a region prospered or was passed over, and whether a new technology was developed or was instead allowed to languish.

Naturally, many resented such fateful power concentrated in a handful of private institutions. Why should the dreams of aspiring entrepreneurs, the homesteads of struggling family farmers, the livelihoods of impoverished industrial workers depend on the imperious whim of some distant New York bank? Moreover, the Wall Street cabal had apparently managed to kidnap the Senate, the Supreme Court, even the presidency itself. The Senate was widely thought of as "the millionaires club," its members representing impersonal corporations rather than flesh-and-blood voters. Henry Demarest Lloyd, whose *Wealth Against Commonwealth* (1894) served as the bible of the anti-monopoly movement, echoed a widely shared conviction that the major political parties were done for: "The Republican Party took the black man off the auction block of the Slave Power, but it has got the white man on the auction block of the Money Power." The nation's highest tribunal had hijacked the 14th Amendment—the Civil War's bloody legacy to the civil liberties of all American citizens—and converted it into a means of protecting corporations against any regulation of their affairs by local and state governments. Every president beginning with Ulysses S Grant opened up the public treasury to railroads and other business interests and made the country's armed forces available when those same circles found themselves under siege by enraged communities. It was

widely noted that in the interregnum separating his two presiden-
cies, Grover Cleveland worked for a Morgan-affiliated law firm.[17]

The Adamses, Charles Francis and Henry, published *Chapters
of Erie* (1871), a devastating indictment of the whole Wall Street
scene. Thinking of Vanderbilt especially, Charles Francis worried about the creation of great financial combines that would
overwhelm the state and its citizenry, gloomily forecasting the
advent of a corporate imperialism. Describing the seduction of
the judiciary, he likened it to a "monstrous parody of the forms of
law; some saturnalia of bench and bar." The whole legislative
process was in immediate danger of being transformed into "a
mart in which the price of votes was haggled over and laws, made
to order, were bought and sold." Although most exercised about
the unchecked power of the railroad barons, the cousins felt that
the integrity of the entire republic was in jeopardy, thanks to a
breed of swindling "moneycrats."[18]

All of this seemed illegitimate; a privileged elite unsanctioned
by law or custom exercising dominion over the commonwealth
smelled suspiciously like an aristocracy. Wall Street especially
seemed to fit this profile. Like that of all previous aristocracies,
its wealth was deemed unearned, leeched from those who toiled
on the country's farms and factories, ships and railroads, from all
those who still kept faith with the moral strictures of the work
ethic. The image of the aristocrat as a noxious parasite was in-
delibly imprinted on the American political consciousness. Wall
Street's arcane and often secretive dealings in mere paper forms

of wealth constituted compelling evidence of its estrangement from the virtuous world of productive labor. Wall Street speculators made up a rentier class on steroids, one that lived not only off the fruit of the land (like feudal lords of old) but off the entire material output and inventive genius of the nation.

So it was that the last third of the nineteenth century was filled with insurgent movements and political parties—the anti-trust movement, the Grange, the Greenback-Labor Party, the Farmers' Alliance and the People's Party, the Knights of Labor, as well as workers' militias and dozens of anarchist and socialist sects—that together singled out Wall Street as the organizer and headquarters of a ruling class, a distinctly un-American and malignant growth on the body politic. In a society dedicated to the proposition that classes did not exist in the New World—or if they did they were fast going out of existence—Wall Street's power was an alarming phenomenon, approaching sacrilege.

One final ingredient made this brew of economic overlordship, backdoor political wire-pulling, aristocratic social pretension, and democratic resentment especially toxic. In Europe it was not uncommon to find aristocrats with a well-developed sense of their social responsibilities. Noblesse oblige or what in Britain came to be known as "Tory socialism" sometimes softened class antagonisms. The breeding and education that went along with heredity privilege could supersede purely self-interested monetary considerations. Even the Federalist gentry adopted this standpoint of disinterested social obligation, although, as was the case with all nobilities, concern for the general interest was never permitted to run up against the needs of the ruling elite. Matters were quite otherwise in late-nineteenth-century America, however.

William Graham Sumner, the Yale sociologist and celebrated proponent of Social Darwinism, published an extended essay in the mid-1880s called *What Social Classes Owe Each Other.* In the new world of free-market competitive capitalism, Sumner argued, the cold hard answer to that question was, "Essentially nothing." Many a newly enriched financier and industrialist emphatically agreed. Those who, like themselves, finished first in the race for survival, were by definition fittest to do so. Since few of these men trailed behind them family traditions, educational accomplishments, careers in public service, or other credentials that might anchor their sudden social preeminence, mountainous piles of cash would do, indeed would have to do. Social Darwinian ideology turned that lone criterion into a moral sufficiency. It served at the same time as a justification for unprecedented and unaccountable power and as consoling eyewash for the less fit. If everyone deferred to the same iron laws of the marketplace, they all would, in the long run, come out ahead—or at least come out where nature had destined them to finish. Progress was assured in this fable, even if its benefits were unevenly distributed. This wondrous system of automatic social regulation perfectly suited the natural instincts of the new tycoonery. Since they wanted nothing to interfere with their moneymaking, they were not inclined to busy themselves with politics, which could be an irritating distraction. Faith in the inexorable mechanics of the free market excused their abdication from public life (except for those lucrative interchanges with the government Land Office and the Treasury Department). It might be said that this was a "ruling class" that, Bartleby-like, preferred not to . . . unless it had to.[19]

As things evolved it did have to. A growing premonition of impending social cataclysm shadowed all sectors of American society beginning not long after the Civil War and culminating in the election of 1896. From the pinnacles of wealth and prestige on Fifth Avenue's Millionaires Mile to the squalid urban barrios and bare-boned sharecropper cabins, people feared that the country was once again dividing in two, that it faced a second civil war while the memory of the first was still fresh in everyone's mind. Only this time a financial aristocracy had supplanted the vanquished slavocracy as the primal threat to the country's democratic and egalitarian birthright. Social upheaval, often accompanied by deadly violence, began with the nationwide railroad strike of 1877 and continued with frightening regularity over the next twenty years. Even today we remember the starkest and most incendiary of those social tragedies: the cruel confrontation in 1885 between Jay Gould and his employees on the Missouri Pacific Railroad when Gould boasted he could hire half the working class to kill the other half; the "Great Uprising" for the eight-hour day and the Haymarket bombing of 1886 that ended with the judicial lynching of the Chicago anarchists; the Homestead Strike of 1892 against Andrew Carnegie's steel works when the

Monongahela River ran red with the blood of Pinkerton strike breakers; the Pullman Strike of 1894 during which George Pullman's utopian exercise in industrial paternalism crashed head-on into the realities of industrial depression, workplace rebellion, and federal bayonets; the populist uprising that spread from the desolate cotton fields of the South to the parched and locust-plagued prairies of the Midwest and promised to "raise less corn and more hell" unless the Wall Street snake was defanged.[20]

In an age characterized by apocalyptic premonitions, the most horrific vision of this final conflict was captured by populist tribune Ignatius Donnelley in his dystopian novel *Caesar's Column* (1891). Along with Edward Bellamy's *Looking Backward* (1888) and Harriet Beecher Stowe's *Uncle Tom's Cabin* (1852), Donnelley's novel was one of the biggest sellers of the nineteenth century. Grim beyond compare, Donnelley's picture of Armageddon even included the logistical details of hunting down the beast in its lair. The Brotherhood of Destruction, a conspiratorial band of brutalized proletarians, driven over the edge by merciless oppression and resentment, initiates its assault on the Oligarchy by barricading the area around Wall Street. This counter-conspiracy succeeds—if success can be measured as a nineteenth-century version of mutual assured destruction—and then the true horror begins. "Caesar's Column" turns out to be an infernal obelisk named in honor of the commanding general of the Brotherhood, Caesar Lomellini. It is a giant pyramid erected in Union Square following the insurrection made out of cement and a quarter of a million corpses of the vanquished Oligarchy and their minions. Built by the forced labor of surviving merchants, politicians, and clergy, it commemorates the "Death and burial of Modern Civilization." To ensure its permanence Caesar's Column is rigged with explosives at its center; should anyone try removing the corpses the monument will blow up.[21]

What this pattern of carnage and irreconcilable confrontation confirmed was that the nouveau aristocracy lacked the training, experience, and ideology (or, for that matter, the inclination) to react in any other way. When faced with challenges to its political, economic, and social presumptions this elite's first and last resort was to one or another kind of blunt instrument. This in turn only exacerbated its reputation as a heartless aristocracy, or, rather, as an aristocracy whose black heart could be found thumping away on Wall Street.

■

The defeat of populism in 1896 signaled a shift in the wind. The election was a decisive victory for the country's business classes. Wall Street, particularly J. P. Morgan, had invested heavily in a Republican triumph, viewing the election as a kind of final conflict between that "awful democracy" and the forces of law and order. The stock market soared soon afterward, indicating its pleasure with the outcome. Then the depression lifted. At the same time, elements within the upper reaches of American business, chastened by the experience of the previous two decades, searched for less inflammatory ways of defending their hegemony. Again, Morgan was chief among them. But try as he and others might they emitted an aroma of aristocratic hauteur no matter what they did.[22]

Two stories about Morgan are telling in this regard. The Morgan bank led the great merger movement at the turn of the century. It had multiple objectives, but chief among them was to end the chaos that was an inescapable feature of internecine competitive capitalism. Folding dozens of separate firms into single consolidated corporations all beholden to and supervised by a gentlemen's club of white-shoe investment bankers would, or so it was assumed, tame the inherent anarchy of the free market. Economic orderliness would in turn quiet the incessant demands for political and social reform. The underlying conceit of this Wall Street regency was that it would steer the economy in the general interest: that it could be trusted to function as a kind of disinterested elite, drawing on its broad knowledge and Olympian vantage point.

Skeptics were everywhere, however. Teddy Roosevelt was first among them. Not long after assuming the presidency following the assassination of William McKinley, he issued a series of jeremiads condemning "malefactors of great wealth" and warning about the "baleful consequences of over-capitalized trusts." A descendant of the old Knickerbocker gentry in colonial and Federalist-era New York, he made no secret of his dubious regard for the captains of finance and industry. He was not about to abdicate his role as the nation's elected chief executive in favor of a self-appointed circle of financiers.[23]

Matters came to a head in the government's prosecution of the Northern Securities Company for violating the Sherman Antitrust Act. Northern Securities was a concoction of the Morgan and Kuhn, Loeb banks, a typical device for bringing to an end a nasty conflict among competing railroads that was proving not only self-destructive but a generator of wider economic instability. When the Justice Department filed its lawsuit, Morgan was irritated. Why, he asked Roosevelt, hadn't the president sent his man to meet with Morgan's factotum to work out the problem in private like two gentlemen? "If we have done anything wrong . . . send your man to my man and they can fix it up." After all, the banker had long ago concluded that "the community of interests" was merely "the principle that certain numbers of men who own property can do what they like with it." Here was the nub of the matter. White-shoe Wall Street implicitly considered itself the president's peer. In this view of the world, Morgan and Roosevelt were to treat each other like two heads of state. The president found this aristocratic presumption intolerable.[24]

While his reputation as a trust-buster has been greatly exaggerated, and while Roosevelt harbored his own elitist distrust of "awful democracy," he acknowledged what Morgan's Wall Street world did not: that anyone exercising broad powers over the public welfare had to be publicly accountable. Roosevelt ignored Morgan's insolence and allowed the lawsuit to proceed, ending in the dissolution of Northern Securities. But the incident only re-affirmed his conviction that although the titans of business and finance might possess great commercial and organizational acumen, that did not qualify them as trustworthy guardians of the nation's well-being. His belief that these financial plutocrats constituted the "most sordid of all aristocracies" was bred in the bone, part of an upbringing that dismissed materialistic strivings as unworthy, debilitating, and even effeminate. He worked at showing respect toward them but confessed: "I am simply unable to make myself take the attitude of respect toward the very wealthy men which such an enormous multitude of people evidently feel. I am delighted to show any courtesy to Pierpont Morgan or Andrew Carnegie or James Hill, but as for regarding any of them as, for instance, I regard . . . Peary, the Arctic explorer, or Rhodes the historian—why I could not force myself to do it even if I wanted to, which I don't."[25]

The irony here was palpable. From the president's vantage point he was the true Brahmin in the best, disinterested sense of that category: someone who was prepared to elevate the national interest above the interests of all other more parochial groups. Morgan was a mere plutocrat concealing his purely mercenary motivations behind a facade of white-shoe sangfroid and statesman-like solemnity. For his part, Morgan reciprocated the president's keen dislike. When Roosevelt set off on his African safari follow-ing his second term in office, Morgan was alleged to have said, "I hope the first lion he meets does his duty."[26]

Both men nurtured illusions about themselves and each other. While he kept up the rhetorical heat, Roosevelt came in time to an understanding with the Wall Street regency and allowed his administration to enter into precisely the kinds of gentlemen's agreements about financial and corporate affairs that Morgan took for granted. Morgan, on the other hand, persisted in think-ing of the president as more of a rabble rouser than he really was. Instead, the most serious assaults on Wall Street's presumptions came from other quarters.

The second story about Morgan involves his encounter with Arsène Pujo, an obscure congressman from Louisiana who in 1912 found himself presiding at the climax of a great national contro-versy over the power of Wall Street. Pujo chaired a congressional investigation into what was notoriously depicted as "the Money Trust." Antitrust sentiments had roiled the waters since the late nineteenth century. John D. Rockefeller's Standard Oil had aroused the most sustained public ire. But during the Progressive era muckraking journalists, politicians, and hard-pressed mer-chants and manufacturers—not to mention struggling farmers and striking workers—had fired away at trusts in every conceiv-able field, from copper and linseed oil to steel and street railways. Towering above them all, however, was the Money Trust, the mother of all trusts. For men like Louis Brandeis, crusading jurist and future Supreme Court Justice, this dense network of investment banks and their financial satellites threatened to crush the life out of economic and political democracy. Brandeis published a series of celebrated exposés in *Harper's* under a rubric, "Other People's Money," which to this day remains a part of our national vocabulary. It was a journalistic tour de force, an armada of data anatomizing the intricate web of connections linking the Wall Street fraternity to the country's major corporations, describing its chokehold over access to capital and economic opportunity for outsiders, and alerting readers to Wall Street's hidden political influence and subversive threat to the democratic process. In language echoing Jefferson and Lincoln, Brandeis went so far as to call the conflict with the Money Trust "irreconcilable," cautioning that "our democracy cannot endure half free and half slave."[27]

Brandeis was also a close confidant of soon-to-be President Woodrow Wilson. The Democratic candidate adopted the muckraking lawyer's point of view and promised throughout his 1912 campaign to take on the Money Trust and prevent it from usurping the democratic birthright of the American people. In his acceptance speech at the Democratic Party convention, Wilson delivered an ominous broadside: "There are not merely great trusts and combinations . . . there is something bigger still . . . more subtle, more evasive, more difficult to deal with. There are vast confederacies of banks, railways, express companies, insurance companies, manufacturing corporations, mining corporations, power and development companies . . . bound together by the fact that the ownership of their stock and members of their boards of directors are controlled and determined by comparatively small and closely interrelated groups of persons who . . . may control, if they please and when they will, both credit and enterprise."[28]

A showdown of sorts occurred at the Pujo hearings. Witnesses from the highest circles of the financial establishment like the "Silver Fox," James Keene, seemed to confirm the existence of the Trust and its extraordinary plenipotentiary authority. George M. Reynolds of the Continental and Commercial National Bank of Chicago confessed, "I believe the money power now lies in the hands of a dozen men. I plead guilty to being one of the dozen."[29]

Others testified adamantly to the contrary, Morgan most famously. His appearance at the Capitol was treated by the media as if he were a visiting dignitary from abroad. Flanked by a battalion of lawyers, partners, and family members, Morgan coolly denied that he possessed any special influence over economic affairs while a standing-room-only crowd looked on entranced. Interrogated by chief counsel Samuel Untermeyer, who came armed with piles of damning documentary evidence, the testimony ran like this:

UNTERMEYER: You do not have any power in any department of industry in this country, do you?

MORGAN: I do not.

UNTERMEYER: Not the slightest?

MORGAN: Not the slightest.

UNTERMEYER: And you are not looking for any?

MORGAN: I am not seeking it either.

UNTERMEYER: This consolidation and amalgamation of systems and industries and banks does not look to any concentration, does it?

MORGAN: No, sir.

UNTERMEYER: It looks, I suppose, to a dispersal of interests rather than to a concentration?

MORGAN: Oh, no, it deals with things as they exist.

On the face of it Morgan's know-nothing obtuseness was plainly preposterous. What also stands out, however, is his self-assurance and studied aloofness, his indifference to this public interrogation, and his genuine conviction that he was member of a financial gentry which conducted its affairs on the basis of trust, a world run by codes of honor where commercial muscularity didn't figure in. Jacob Schiff, Morgan's near equivalent at Kuhn, Loeb, took a different tack, admitting the concentration of power but finding it no cause for worry: that power, he claimed, was in "good hands." These men saw themselves as the living embodiments of precisely that aristocratic caste which many found infuriating but which they themselves knew in their hearts to be benign.[30]

Morgan died just months after the Pujo Committee concluded its affairs. Despite the hearings and the long decade of political denunciation of Wall Street's transgressions that preceded them, the passing of the financier was likened to the loss of a Shakespeare or a Lincoln. "J. P. Morgan will rank in the history of the Republic as one of the greatest men God has yet raised to serve it," eulogized the Reverend William Wilkinson in the somber stillness of Trinity Church. So, too, the world he represented continued its iconic career as the country's unofficial aristocracy, not a beloved one but admired, feared, and deferred to enough to sustain its preeminence until a crisis descended over the nation that was grave enough to unseat it.[31]

■

The Great Depression was that crisis. Only the Civil War presented a greater traumatic shock to the nation's psyche, not to mention its material well-being. Whether the stock market crash of 1929 was responsible for the total economic collapse that followed has been debated by historians and economists ever since. For the generation that lived through this cataclysm, however, there was no doubt that Wall Street was guilty as sin. All the suspicion and animosity that had accumulated since Jefferson's day descended on the Street.

In his first inaugural address, Franklin Delano Roosevelt announced that "the money changers have fled from their high seats in the temple of our civilization." Those "unscrupulous money changers," he confidently averred, "stood indicted in the court of public opinion, rejected by the hearts and minds of men." In his first "fireside chat," he promised to pursue a final reckoning with the illegitimate and overbearing financial aristocracy that had shadowed the nation since at least the days of Andrew Jackson. "The day of the great promoter or the financial titan to whom we granted everything, if only he would build or develop, is over." Invoking the language of the Pujo Money Trust investigations to excoriate his enemies, the president confirmed a suspicion running back to the Gilded Age that "fewer than three dozen private banking houses and stock selling adjuncts in the commercial banks have directed the flow of capital in the country and outside it." Along the way they had erected pyramids of watered stock, milked subsidiaries, and choked off new avenues of property holding and mobility.[32]

FDR possessed a more genial temperament than his fire-and-brimstone cousin Theodore, one less imperious and bullying. But their regard for the plutocracy was the same. Like Teddy, Franklin hailed from the world of Hudson River valley gentleman farmers; he knew a true aristocrat when he saw one, and the men from Wall Street did not qualify. The president wrote to his close adviser, "brains-trust" member Adolph Berle, that "the fundamental trouble with this whole stock exchange crowd is their complete lack of elementary education. I do not mean lack of college diplomas, etc. but just inability to understand the country or public or their obligations to their fellow men. Perhaps you

can help them acquire a kindergarten knowledge of these subjects. More power to you." Roosevelt was prepared, with a great
deal of political tacking, to put the pretenders in their place.[33]

The severity of the crisis made that possible. Wall Street had
proved itself not only ethically challenged and dangerously om-
nipotent but, more damning than that, omni-incompetent. During the boom years of the 1920s, the white-shoe world of J. P.
Morgan had accepted credit for the nation's good fortune and
been portrayed as a conclave of wise men. Now, under the new circumstances of economic ruination, that same world was treated as
criminally irresponsible, pathetic even, an object not only of censure but of mockery. And there is perhaps nothing more fatal for
the life expectancy of an elite than to be viewed as ridiculous.

Defrocking the Wall Street regency was a pastime enjoyed by
many. The president's excoriating rhetoric was seconded by congressional investigations which embarrassed the most dignified
financiers and turned up multiple cases of financial whistling in
the dark, malfeasance, and sheer larceny. Senators fumed about
the way "the lambs have been sheared" by the "rascals on Wall
Street"; others compared Wall Street's inner circles to the gang-
land world of Al Capone. Father Charles Coughlin, the charismatic and notoriously anti-Semitic radio priest from Detroit,
with millions of listeners, ridiculed "the divine intelligence of the
international bankers," which, he proclaimed, "has found its deserved place with the theory of the divine right of kings. Both are
putrid corpses." The populist demagogic governor of Louisiana,

Huey Long, railed against bloated, sybaritic plutocrats. Early on in the New Deal he charged that the Treasury Department had fallen into the clutches of the House of Morgan and the "heeled headman of Wall Street Bernard Baruch." Meanwhile, New Deal legislation—the Glass-Steagall Act (the Banking Act of 1933), securities laws including the creation of the Securities and Exchange Commission, the Wealth Tax Act, the Public Utility Holding Company Act—established public supervision and regulation of the Money Trust. Brandeis's bête noire came away weakened if not exactly leveled.[34]

Journalists and practical jokers had a field day. Edmund Wilson sketched an acidly humorous portrait of onetime Wall Street legend "Sunshine Charlie." Charles Mitchell had been president of the National City Bank, the country's largest. He was the mastermind of the bank's headfirst plunge into the mass marketing of Wall Street during the Jazz Age and won a reputation as a financial guru. But in the aftermath of the crash word leaked out that it was also Mitchell, that "banker of bankers," who had played fast and loose with depositors' funds, investing them in wobbly stocks and bonds that the bank's investment affiliate was busy hawking. It was Sunshine Charlie who had speculated in the stock of his own bank. In court the man who had inspired awe looked "cheap." His ruddy face, his high stiff collar, blue serge suit, and white breast-pocket handkerchief were all that was left of "those millennial boasts of the bankers, the round-eyed hopes of the public." His sangfroid evaporated on the witness stand.

Mitchell broke down in the middle of sentences, his pointing finger robbed of its former conviction and power to command. From Wilson's vantage point, Sunshine Charlie belonged to a species of imperial fakes: "Enormous with no necks, they gave the impression of hooked, helpless frogs, or fat bass or leggy groupers hauled suddenly out of the water and landed on the witness stand gasping."[35]

Of course the House of Morgan was a favorite target. In one instance, Jack Morgan, who had run the bank since his father's death, arrived in Washington to be grilled by congressional inquisitors. Lost in his own oblivious self-regard, he made unintentional fun of himself and the hermetically sealed world he came from. Following his testimony he lectured reporters: "If you destroy the leisure class, you destroy civilization. By the leisure class I mean families who employ one servant, twenty-five to thirty million families." Delighted with this factoid, commentators rushed to their typewriters and microphones to report Morgan's wacky view of the nation's domestic life, pointing out that the 1930 census revealed there were fewer than thirty million families in the whole country, and, sadly, fewer than two million cooks and servants to tend to them.[36]

As it turned out, hapless Jack's roasting was hardly over with. At another appearance before Congress, and before he could even begin testifying, just as he was getting himself settled, surrounded by advisers, family, and a horde of newspapermen and radio commentators, a young, rather attractive midget, one Lya Graff, was plopped down in the august banker's lap, placed there by two PR flaks with profoundly bad taste and an acute sense of how the times were changing. Photographs of the portly, bushy-eyed, white-mustachèd banker, a look of bemusement on his face, Miss Graff perched beatifically on his knee, circled the globe. It was a small but transformative moment in popular culture; the epitome of aristocratic banker villainy was suddenly made to appear about as dangerous as an old fogy. The House of Morgan, more than any other establishment, had been the emblem of Wall Street dignity, wisdom, and statesmanship for three generations. When Lya Graff cozied up on Jack's lap that aura evaporated in a burst of laughter that dissolved the intimidating solemnity and exclusivity of the Morgan bank and the elite conclave it stood for.[37]

■

Wall Street's iconic status as the nation's enduring emblem of aristocracy came to an end with the New Deal. The ignominy heaped upon it was deep and long-lasting, so much so that it faded from view as a central metaphor in the nation's political imagery, no longer the magnetic center around which the political symbolism of rich and poor, class versus class, orbited. When that long silence did finally end, beginning in the Reagan era, Wall Street had undergone a makeover. It no longer wore the face of the aristocrat but on the contrary came forward as a rebel against the establishment. Michael Milken, Carl Icahn, Ivan Boesky, and others fancied themselves and were treated by the media as warriors against sclerotic corporate management, hyper-cautious, elitist financiers in pinstripes and pince-nez, and suffocating, overly nosy government bureaucrats.

Wall Street would be accused of many wrongdoings in the years to come. Milken and others would serve time in jail once the junk bond merger and acquisition mania of the 1980s ran its course. A decade later *Enronization* entered the national vocabulary after the bursting of the dot.com bubble; a new noun to capture a level of white-collar criminal chicanery by the nation's corporate and financial elite that would have astonished William Duer. So too, a degree of extravagantly conspicuous consumption—the *New York Times Magazine* annual "Fashions of the Times" gushed after Reagan's inaugural ball that "at long last" luxury was back—and gross disparities in the social division of income and wealth turned the Reagan era into a second Gilded Age. But with an odd-ball exception here and there, the new tycoonery did not fancy itself an aristocracy, did not dress up like or marry its daughters off to European nobility. On the contrary, it dressed down, in blue jeans, and affected a faux populism or nerdy dishevelment in the way it presented itself. Although the political power of Wall Street was arguably as great as or even greater than it had been in the halcyon days of J. P. Morgan, both the Street and the country's political culture had evolved. Fear of a moneyed aristocracy, which had first alarmed Jefferson and continued to fire up political emotions for another century and a half, was apparently a thing of the past.[38]

Wall Street's career as a stand-in for an American aristocracy had never felt quite right anyway. The Street's single-minded fixation on moneymaking made it too irreverent, too chronically unsettled to harbor a true aristocracy, one bound by tradition and fixed social position. Anger directed its way secretly or not so secretly reflected more the country's anxieties about the precariousness and inequities of capitalism, less its real fear of some feudal counterrevolution. Moreover, when William Duer or Sunshine Charlie Mitchell behaved badly, they resembled something deep in the American grain more than they did titled aristocrats. Supremely confident men and alluring ones, they were also given to overreaching, secrecy, and deceit, and to living on the borders of illegality. Over the years Wall Street gave off the seductive yet sinister aroma of the confidence man.

The Confidence Man

Mark Twain once described a mine as "a hole in the ground with a liar standing next to it," which neatly summed up his attitude toward Wall Street: it was not to be trusted. And as a matter of fact, just around the time Twain voiced his cynicism about the country's penchant for financial high-jinks in his first best-selling novel, *The Gilded Age*, written with Charles Dudley Warner, newspaper readers everywhere were mesmerized by the story of the Great Diamond Hoax of 1872.[1]

Bogus gold and silver mines had been springing up all over the place, but this was the biggest fraud to hit the American West. Two confidence men—Philip Arnold from Harlan County, Kentucky, who had done some small-time gold prospecting in California, and his partner, "Silent" John Slack—ran the operation, taking advantage of the chronic outsized optimism prevalent among

prospectors and investors back East, as well as of the recent discovery of diamonds in South Africa. The partners boned up on
their technical knowledge of diamonds, put together a sackful
of uncut jewels purchased in London, and concocted a story
about a mother lode they had come across in Apache territory in
Arizona. The sack and the story were enough to rope in a couple
of San Francisco bankers (one of them a former wild-cat mine
promoter and filibuster in Nicaragua). Arnold and Slack convinced them that sizable capital was required to mount an armed
expedition to secure and exploit the cache. Not entirely gullible,
these initial investors insisted on some proof of the mine's existence. In response, Arnold and Slack concocted an elaborate
ruse that included taking the blindfolded bankers' agent on a
long trek into the wilderness, ending up a few miles outside Den-
ver. There the confidence men had seeded a mesa with various
precious stones that the agent dug up with his fingernails. In a
state of high excitement, he reported back to his employers that
Arnold and Slack had discovered an "American Golconda."

Now New York money became interested. A corporate lawyer,
General Benjamin Butler (a powerful congressman), and two of
the nation's most prestigious investment bankers, August Belmont and Henry Seligman, formed a group to pursue the project, appointing General George B. McClellan (commander of
the Army of the Potomac until Lincoln fired him for his passivity) as the new company's figurehead, hoping thus to inspire further confidence in the undertaking. What residual skepticism re-

mained was eliminated when Charles Tiffany, the country's most renowned jewelry expert, testified to the mine's bona fides. Tiffany was a bit of a blowhard who had begun his business career as a Yankee notions peddler and knew precious little about uncut stones. But he had what so many of his on-the-make countrymen shared: a superabundant confidence in himself and the American cornucopia, and a great capacity for self-delusion. With Tiffany, Belmont (the Rothschilds' agent in America), and McClellan involved, Arnold and Slack had no trouble collecting well over half a million dollars (a very handsome sum in those days) in "earnest money" for their "labors." They then decamped to Quebec, where they gathered some new gems with which to re-seed the mesa. A new exploratory expedition dug up the seeded jewels with shovels, and the delirious news drifted back East that the mesa would yield $5 million per acre and contained 3,000 acres. Wall Street went crazy. The San Francisco and New York Mining and Commercial Company began its short life by issuing 100,000 shares, and from Paris, Baron Rothschild sententiously observed, "America is a rich land. It has given us many surprises. It reserves many more."

Surprises indeed! Soon enough the confidence game was exposed by Clarence King, a government geologist and close friend of Henry Adams's. He wrote to the board of directors to tell them that "the diamond fields upon which are based such large investment and such brilliant hope are utterly valueless," and that the investors were the victims of "an unparalleled fraud."

Meanwhile Silent John Slack disappeared. Arnold returned to his Kentucky homestead, where he remained wealthy and became a sort of local hero for putting one over on the Wall Street Yankees. Later, however, he overreached—always a fatal flaw in the makeup of the confidence man—and tried starting a bank to compete with a local nabob. He received a shotgun blast in the back of the head for his temerity.[2]

■

The confidence man is endemic to market society. First of all this is because market society rests on confidence: confidence that strangers can be relied upon to live up to agreements, made often at long distance and extending over long periods of time; confidence too that contractual relationships will bind people together on the basis of mutual self-interest. The confidence man trades in that trust, takes advantage of it. His basic traits are familiar to us all. He is charming, glib, seductive, even charismatic, often sexy. He is a trickster, to be sure. But what is most notable is that his trick depends on the willing collaboration of his victim, or mark. The mark indulges in an act of faith born out of cupidity: the belief that there is a way to fast money that skirts the rigors and renunciations of the work ethic. *Cupidity* is a loaded word. The mark's motivation may be ingenuous, idealistic even, amounting to a buoyant optimism about the future. Still, even the most innocent approach the confidence man with a certain foreboding: something feels not quite right, something illicit hovers nearby, something echoes danger—but that same something is very hard to resist.

Confidence men appear particularly at the frontier zones of market society, at those times and places where the unknown beckons even as it frightens. Capitalism, in its surges of creative destruction, is always producing new frontier zones, fields of such expansive opportunity they are virtually impossible to map. Just because they are boundless, they present raw material for the commercial imagination as well as the criminal imagination of the confidence man. Confidence men show up throughout the history of Wall Street. In the world of the Street, where speculators live in a limbolike state of permanent impermanence, a weird, alluring, menacing landscape without end or resting place, there is always an open invitation to the confidence man.

During certain moments in American history, however, confidence men seem to breed in alarming numbers. Or at least the level of popular preoccupation with their presence rises noticeably. Twain tracked them during the Gilded Age. The Jazz Age of the 1920s and the dot.com mania of the 1990s were similarly overrun. Strikingly, these periods coincided with high levels of technological innovation, with a kind of techno-futurism that promised not just some new gadgetry but a whole new way of life. For the Jazz Age that was best represented by aeronautics and the radio; in the 1990s by the Internet. In such eras mere matters of dollars and cents are transmogrified, become incongruous forms of commercial exaltation, drawing on subterranean energies that are not part of the normal trucking and bartering of market society. A kind of giddiness pervades the air, an atmosphere of excitement, of living large and dangerously—the oxygen on which the confidence man thrives.

America's baptismal experience with the topsy-turvy world of the confidence man occurred a generation before Twain's prevaricating mine promoters appeared on the scene, in the Jacksonian era. If it is right to say that confidence men crop up on the frontiers of market society, then it is arguably the case that the whole country represented such a frontier in the antebellum years. It was then that a society based on the marketplace began its long march through the corridors of American life. The rise of the paper economy was a particularly strange and forbidding development. Banknotes, bonds, mortgages, bills of exchange, and stocks seemed to form a spider web of poisonous paper, ensnaring and devouring the hard-earned fruits of honest labor. Intangible, yet powerful, this paper system produced social, even intellectual vertigo. It unsettled all previously existing social relations: family lineages, ancient homesteads, local loyalties, honored occupations, patriarchal deference, venerable institutions of church and community, cherished beliefs about the natural sources of wealth and the springs of virtue—all that had served to fix identities of person and place for generations. All this and more could be instantly disordered, deranged by the madness of an economy that was no more stable and enduring than the paper it chased after. Upheavals were felt on the land, in towns, and in the city.

Alongside and endemic to this commercial upheaval the country underwent a veritable orgy of speculation: in new lands, in the canals and turnpikes and railroads of the transportation revolution, in the infrastructure of the water-borne mercantile economy, in new towns and cities that seemed to spring up overnight (at least in the imaginations of their promoters). For people with either limited or no contact with the marketplace and its impersonal relationships—its indifference to customary ways of doing things, all values not readily monetized, and moral prohibitions that got in the way of business—the world began to feel stranger, more fluid, promising yet uncertain. Jacksonian America overflowed with confidence about the future of the country, a much-celebrated indigenous national character trait that only the most traumatic blows—the Civil War, the Great Depression—could deflate. Yet it was obsessed with the confidence man. In a word, Jacksonian Americans experienced a great crisis of confidence.

Some observers took the measure of this new risk-prone way of life and pronounced it good. Washington Irving, for example, who for a long time deplored the awakening spirit of avaricious self-seeking, later discovered its metaphysical justification. Mere trade might be grubby and pedestrian, but speculation was its "romance. . . . It renders the stock jobber a magician and the [stock] exchange a region of enchantment." Irving himself became a propagandist for the western imperial schemes of John Jacob Astor and a speculator in railroads and land, in which he lost heavily. In his own way, Ralph Waldo Emerson agreed with

Irving. While he resented the new order of things that deferred to wealth and nothing else, he drew a connection between the popular passion for speculative risk taking and what he considered the American genius for enterprise, innovation, and great projects. Even Horace Greeley, who could turn apoplectic about the depravity of gambling, nonetheless found it in him to offer up an apologia for speculation as inherent in the national character and expressive of a democratic social order, a form of equal opportunity open to the bold.[3]

Ordinary folk like Jeremiah Church saw things the same way. He noted in his diary that in America, "everyman [*sic*] is a speculator from a wood-sawyer to a President, as far as his means will go, and credit also." In one way or another, he and many of his fellow citizens were swept away by what was quickly becoming a national faith, reiterated endlessly in newspaper editorials, political stump speeches, a burgeoning self-help literature, and the everyday promotional rhetoric of commercial life: that what really distinguished the American spirit was its audacity, its eagerness to venture into the unknown, its inspiring confidence that what lay beyond the borders of the familiar was bound to be good, not only for the individual seeking his fortune but also for a nation growing more muscular and with its eyes on glory.[4]

Confidence this outsized left the nation ripe for the picking, though the harvesting might be relatively benign. Americans began congratulating themselves on a certain native capacity for commercial guile captured in the figure of the peddler "Yankee

Jonathan." He looked a bit like Uncle Sam—lean, angular, sly but friendly—and was charming, full of folktales and good humor. He had a way with country wives and knew how to strike a sharp bargain but stopped just this side of the felonious. A more malignant figure, however, began to command attention. Confidence men were abroad in the land, concocting and hawking illusory agricultural Arcadias, gossamer towns and paper cities, bone-dry canals to nowhere, railroad lines consisting of "two streaks of rust," as the popular phrase had it.

Charles Dickens (who traveled to the United States in 1842 and disliked most of what he saw, especially the rampant money mania of New York) provided one of the most searing and hilarious depictions of the fatuousness and hypocrisy that lurked beneath the surface of this romance of risk. Martin Chuzzlewit, the hapless hero of the novel of the same name, is seduced by the huckstering riffs of New York land promoters—an irresistible blend of high-falutin' democratic egalitarianism and unblinkered covetousness—almost as soon as he gets off the boat from England. Martin asks "The General," the confidence man who entices him to invest in his cleverly named Eden Land Corporation, if there is anything in his scheme for the buyers. Puffing himself up impressively the General replies: "For the buyers, sir? . . . Well! you come from an old country, from a country, sir, that has piled up golden calves as high as Babel and worshipped 'em for ages. We are a new country, sir; man is in a more primeval state here, sir; we have not the excuse of having lapsed in the slow course of time into degenerate practices; we have no false gods; man, sir, here, is man in all his dignity. We fought for that or nothing. Here am I sir, . . . with gray hairs, sir, and a moral sense. Would I, with my principles, invest capital in this speculation if I didn't think it full of hopes and chances for my brother man? . . . What are the Great United States for, sir, . . . if not for the regeneration of man? But it is nat'ral for you to make such an enquerry for you come from England and you do not know my country." Soon afterward, shown a map depicting "banks, churches, cathedrals, market-places, factories, hotels, stores, mansions, wharves, an exchange, a theater, public buildings of all kinds," Martin takes the plunge and invests his meager capital in the Eden Land Corporation, only to discover, after schlepping out to a remote corner of Illinois, that Eden is nothing more than a hellish, fetid swamp, where Martin nearly loses his life, not to mention his life savings.[5]

Wall Street was not yet at the center of this vertiginous new world. Dealings on the recently created (1817) New York Stock and Exchange Board involved a tiny number of people. It was out in the countryside where the new obsession with speculating on a rising market took root. The era is infamous for wagering on the commercial future of new lands and the farms and towns that were supposed to spring up there and sometimes did, but often did not. Indeed, matters grew so out of control that they led to a devastating depression, which lasted from 1837 into the early 1840s. Wall Street was certainly implicated, the precipitating event being the fatal overreaching of a rather conservative New York financial institution. But what is most relevant is that the Street soon emerged as a site, and an increasingly prominent one, where people wrestled with this more widespread crisis of confidence.

The city, new to the American scene, fascinated people then as a realm of mystery and transgression. Wall Street was of course a quintessentially city place. George Foster, who became perhaps the best-known chronicler of the urban demimonde in the antebellum years, sketched the urban scene in his *New York by Gaslight* (1850), which included expeditions onto the Street. Foster and others painted the Street in lurid colors, seeing it at bottom as a site of depravity, but they were alert enough to the crosscurrents of popular emotion to recognize how alluring it was to many. The dream of instant wealth was part of that allure. But Wall Street's inscrutable doings, its flirtation with the illicit, and its crossing over the boundaries of conventional morality generated their own attraction. Foster and other amateur anthropologists of the urban experience provided their readers with a sneaky thrill. They likened the Street to the valley of riches depicted in the tale of Sinbad the Sailor, "where millions of diamonds lay glistening like fiery snow, but which was guarded on all sides by poisonous serpents, whose bite was death and whose contact was pollution." The Street beckoned as "a place of deep and dangerous mystery, a region of dens and caves and labyrinths full of perils." For Foster the Street was above all a boulevard of masquerade and hidden realities, a zone of tempting transgression, romantic but full of risk.[6]

A criminal case that would be considered so ordinary today that it probably would be ignored by the newspapers became a national sensation in 1849. A confidence man, one William Thompson, operating in New York, gulled his victims into believing that if they lent him a valuable belonging—a gold watch, for example—he would let them in on a surefire but highly secret deal. His pitch—common in this line of work—stressed that what was important was not the monetary value of whatever his marks were loaning him but rather its significance as a token of their confidence in him, which in turn would give him confidence in them. This is the classic psychic economy of the confidence game. Eventually Thompson was arrested. He became famous overnight as "the Confidence Man," written about in newspapers and periodicals all across the country. He was an early form of celebrity, who really enjoyed his sudden notoriety, happy to grant interviews from his jail cell in New York's notorious and aptly named "Tombs." He was also Exhibit A for demonstrating how fascinated people had become with the confidence man, and how worried they were even as they indulged in their new passion for speculation. Some Pollyanna-ish types actually found in the Thompson case confirmation of the indefatigable optimism of the American spirit. Others were less sanguine. And so the confidence man became emblematic of a suspicion that would shadow Wall Street for generations to come.

One newspaper account is worth inspecting more closely. First it lets us see why when some people turned their gaze to Wall

Street they saw there the face of the confidence man. More than that, it is an early and vivid, even overwrought, expression of what would become a long-lived piece of Wall Street cultural iconography, the conflation of the image of the aristocrat with that of the confidence man, a conflation that worked to subvert the Street's loftier claims to social esteem.

James Gordon Bennett, the publisher of the *New York Herald*, a pioneer of sensationalist journalism, and a precursor of William Randolph Hearst, used the occasion of Thompson's arrest to anathematize the Street. He was brutally direct. Thompson was a petty swindler. But "those palazzos, with all their costly furniture and all their splendid equipages, have been the produce of the same genius in their proprietors, which made the 'Confidence Man' immortal and a prisoner at 'the Tombs.' His genius has been employed on a small scale in Broadway. Theirs has been employed in Wall Street. . . . He has obtained half a dozen watches. They have pocketed millions of dollars." Bennett questioned the country's moral compass. Thompson "is a swindler. They are exemplars of honesty. He is a rogue. They are financiers. He is collared by the police. They are cherished by society. He is a mean, beggarly, timid, narrow-minded wretch. . . . They are respectable people, princely, bold, high-soaring 'operators,' who are satisfied only with the plunder of the whole community." Thompson ended up in jail rather than some "fashionable fauborg" because he aimed too low. He should have gone to Albany instead and secured himself a railroad charter or issued a "flaming prospectus of another grand scheme. . . . He should have brought the stockholders into bankruptcy" and then "returned to a life of ease, the possessor of a clear conscience, and one million dollars." But the hapless Thompson wasn't up to it, so "let him rot, then, in 'the Tombs' . . . while the genuine 'Confidence Man' stands one of the Corinthian Columns of society. . . . Success, then, to the real 'Confidence Man.' Long life to the real 'Confidence Man' . . . the 'Confidence Man' of Wall Street—the 'Confidence Man' of the Palace uptown."[7]

James Gordon Bennett traded in demagoguery. Herman Melville did not. But they shared a mordant fascination with an emerging commercial civilization which seemed fraudulent at its core. Melville's was a remorseless gaze. That vision achieved a certain black density in what is certainly his most allusive and recondite novel, *The Confidence Man: His Masquerade*. It has been alleged that the germ of the idea for the novel was inspired by William Thompson's notorious arrest. True or not, the book is a veritable compendium of confidence men: religious and philosophical confidence men, literary and political confidence men, crooked businessmen and crooked philanthropists, peddlers of nostrums and miracle cures for the ailments of body and soul, all masquerading together on the steamboat *Fidele* as it floats down the arterial heart of the country, the Mississippi River.

Among the passengers, predictably, is a speculator, experienced in the ways of the stock market. He encounters a young man to whom he seeks to sell stock in the Black Rapids Coal Company.

Negotiations shrouded in mystery proceed; tempting allusions are made to the stock's unavailability, suggesting its preciousness. The young man turns out to be less callow than he seemed and skeptically inquires about why the stock's price has been depressed of late. The speculator–confidence man blames it on the "growling, the hypocritical growling, of the bears." Why "hypocritical," the young man asks. Now the modality of the negotiation shifts; it becomes a metaphysical jeremiad against speculation delivered in the interests of speculation. It is a send-up of Emerson's optimism, of a more pervasive culture of optimism. "Why the most monstrous of all hypocrites are these bears: hypocrites by inversion; hypocrites by all the simulation of dark instead of bright; souls that thrive, less upon depression, than the fiction of depression; professors of the wicked art of manufactured depression, spurious Jeremiahs . . . who, the lugubrious day done, return, like some sham Lazarus among the beggars, to make merry over the gains got by their pretended sore heads . . . scoundrel bears!" Bears, like gloomy philosophers, are destroyers of confidence, avers the speculator, "Fellows who, whether in stocks, politics, bread-stuffs, morals, metaphysics, religion—be what it may—trump up their black panics in the naturally quiet-brightness solely with a view to some sort of covert advantage."

With this reasoning the young man is in perfect emotional sympathy, as are, presumably, most of his countrymen in their quest, undertaken in guilty innocence, for the main chance. His confidence won—he naturally gravitates to "fellows that talk

comfortably and prosperously, like you"—the young man saun-
ters off to conclude the transaction, not, however, in the "bright
sunlight," but in a "private little haven" hidden from view. And
there the game continues as the speculator–confidence man, his
thirst for mercenary deceit unquenchable, entices his young con-
vert with talk of stock in a "New Jerusalem, a new and thriving
city, so called, in northern Minnesota."[8]

By the 1870s, Wall Street had become a regular stop for tourists
to the city, mentioned in all the travel guides not only because of
its growing economic throw weight but because it was becoming
a more and more conspicuous arena in which what might be
called a "risk society" acted out its ambivalence, ready to chance
all but anxious about being deceived. Even as the established exchanges in New York and Chicago, especially, became more imposing, rule bound, and presumably on the up-and-up, an underground, delusional economy flourished, exploiting the cravings
of would-be or used-to-be big-time speculators. "Bucket shops"
were walk-in-off-the-street, one-room affairs in small cities and
towns across the country, housed in dingy, ill-lit, dilapidated buildings, and equipped with a ticker and chalkboard. Gathered there
was a picturesque brotherhood of greed, bound together by fevered
emotions and small passions: a man with a "tip" from a "Trolley
insider" or an unassuming barber who had happened to trim the
beard of some "Napoleon of finance" or perhaps an eccentric

loaded down with elaborate charts of some infallible mathematical system; characters of infinite hope and desperation, a confidence man's delight. Bucket shops (also known colloquially as "funeral parlors") conducted a shady business wagering on the ups and downs of stock prices, often without any stock changing hands, and frequently without the benefit of a real wire reporting real prices of real securities, run by pretend brokers unconnected to any stock or commodity exchange, who rigged the local market until suspicions heated up and they fled into the night.[9]

Wall Street tried to keep its distance from this subterranean world. It even lobbied to outlaw these fringe establishments. But much of what went on among the Street's most conspicuous movers and shakers so closely resembled the confidence rackets of the bucket-shop operators that for many it was a distinction without a difference. One heartrending case involved Civil War hero and former president Grant at a time when he was both deathly ill and verging on poverty. Grant had been gulled into a fraudulent investment scheme run by his guileless son, Ulysses "Buck" Grant, Jr., and a wily Wall Street speculator, Ferdinand Wood, a man of "an insinuating and plausible demeanor." When the firm failed, so too did the rest of the Street, and the nation's favorite general was left a bankrupt.[10]

This coming together of financial hanky-panky and great doings was particularly the case when it came to the railroads, the technocultural equivalent of the Internet during the Gilded Age. No sector of the economy invited more speculative fervor. The roads were bound up with the manifest destiny of the country, promising to link the coasts, settle and civilize great tracts of wilderness, and provide the iron sinews of a continental empire. Consequently, they inspired sound as well as addle-brained commercial schemes and dreams. The railroads were also enormous enterprises requiring great infusions of outside capital. Because Wall Street pooled together and mobilized much of the country's liquid capital, it functioned as the midwife for the birth and development of the nation's principal means of transportation. This combination of great expectations and financial dependency was ripe for exploitation, including forms of exploitation that hovered close to or sometimes crossed the border into illegality, or at least into the shadowy world of the confidence game.

Jay Cooke was without question the most widely respected banker in America during and after the Civil War. His reputation was securely anchored in the national mythos, where he was heralded as a special kind of patriot for keeping the Union solvent by single-handedly disposing of the government's war bonds. It would be hard to exaggerate the high regard for Jay Cooke at the end of the Civil War. He had become a confidant of presidents, a war hero whose sense of duty and financial integrity were universally acclaimed.

But then he embarked on his grandest undertaking, the creation of the Northern Pacific Railroad, which promised to blaze a path through the vast, untracked wilderness of the American Northwest. It was a daunting project, launched with the best of intentions. Soon enough, however, its prospects darkened. The vastness and complexity of the road required enormous sums of money, both public and private. Cooke relied on political influentials to pump up enthusiasm. After completing a portion of the railroad, up to the Red River (so that it wouldn't seem purely chimerical), he petitioned the government for land grants and bond guarantees, in part to induce European immigrants to settle along the route, in part to persuade wealthy continental investors to buy the company's bonds. (The capital of North Dakota was called Bismarck because Cooke was trying to peddle bonds in Germany.) His claims for the road's progress and future prospects became more and more extravagant. It would be a great civilizing project that would populate the wilderness, carrying people and ideas and goods into a rich and unexploited part of the continent. Along with Northern Pacific bonds his sales agents carried maps, posters, and pamphlets extolling the bonanza to come. Celebrities were taken on excursions; traveling exhibits of products from the hinterland were staged around the country.

Slowly the aroma of corruption filtered through. Stories of fraud and thievery surfaced. There were derisive allusions to "Jay Cooke's Banana Belt," mocking the promotional literature that portrayed the region's arid emptiness as a lush tropical paradise. Cooke found himself dangerously overextended. The collapse of Northern Pacific securities in 1873 was responsible, more than any other single event, for the next great Wall Street panic and the most severe depression of the nineteenth century. All the hoopla surrounding the hyping of the railroad—the celebrity testimonials, the patriotic cant about progress and the taming of the continent, the lavishly illustrated, fantastical brochures depicting Duluth as the Paris of the Prairies, the expeditions to Vienna and other European capitals to drum up bond sales and immigrant settlers for hypothetical towns in a tropical outback—all this now seemed like a malignant form of make-believe concocted by a patriot turned confidence man.[11]

Other notorious Wall Street railroad financiers, though with less imposing reputations than Cooke's, encouraged a similar overzealousness among potential investors and sometimes indulged in conspiratorial acts designed to cheat them. The names of Cornelius ("the Commodore") Vanderbilt, "Jubilee Jim" Fisk (also known as "the Admiral"), Daniel Drew (referred to far and wide as "Unc'l Dan'l"), and Jay ("the Mephistopheles of Wall Street") Gould are legendary. These men speculated in railroads with a vengeance, most lavishly the Erie Railroad, notorious as the "scarlet woman of Wall Street." They were associated with the primordial age of the Robber Barons, the country's true immersion into the Industrial Revolution, and they were identified in particular with Wall Street's formative role in that upheaval. As their monikers suggest—grandiloquent, folksy, and cartoonish but with a touch of evil—they had about them the aura of the confidence man. And as a matter of fact, they began their careers in ways not far removed from the sort of dealings Dickens's General and Melville's riverboat speculator trafficked in. As young men Fisk and Drew both spent their time earning a living in traveling circuses, learning the con games common there. The Mephistophelean Gould was alleged to have made his initial stake cheating a partner in the tannery business, driving the poor fellow to suicide. And "the Commodore" started as a ferry-boat captain, a legitimate enough business, but was well known as a razor-sharp wheeler and dealer with minimal scruples.

During the "Erie wars," these men resorted to every imaginable device and stratagem. When Drew, Fisk, and Gould faced off against the Commodore for control of the Erie, they brazenly printed up as much stock as was necessary to keep their enemy at bay. Company reports, to the degree these men even deigned to issue them, were full of lies, half-lies, and gross omissions, particularly regarding the decrepit state of the Erie. British investors later spent decades suing the road to recover funds these Wall Street titans had in effect absconded with. When Fisk and Gould tried to corner the market in gold, they nearly succeeded, in part by circulating made-up stories about President Grant's plans to hoard some of the Treasury Department's gold stock so as to boost the prices abroad for American farm products. Like many a confidence man, they often found themselves outrunning the law or a posse of enraged investors. When the "corner in gold" collapsed crowds gathered, hoping to catch a glimpse of the renegade conspirators. Spotted, Fisk and Gould were chased through the streets to Jubilee Jim's Grand Opera House, where they lived under siege for days. During the Erie wars Fisk and

Gould, along with Unc'l Dan'l Drew, compelled the Commodore to engorge limitless quantities of Erie stock at ever escalating prices, which his rivals were simply printing up at will. When Vanderbilt bribed a pliant judge to issue a warrant for the arrest of Gould and Fisk, the two shanghaied a small skiff at midnight just in time to make a fog-enshrouded and nearly catastrophic voyage across New York Harbor to a safe haven on the Jersey shore, the cops in hot pursuit.[12]

All this derring-do, subterfuge, and artful dodging were combined with conventional business practices—sharp financial dealings to be sure, but otherwise normal and legal, if not exactly exemplary. And that is just the point. These men were not operating bucket shops. To the contrary, they were among the most respected, if feared, men on Wall Street; it would be fair to say they personified the Street. Yet their apparent lack of scruple, their willingness, even eagerness to hoodwink the public, strongly suggested in the eyes of many that the Street itself was running a confidence game.

About this Mark Twain had no doubt. He knew it in his bones in part because he was himself the perfect mark, very much a kindred spirit of Melville's young man on the *Fidele*. Twain was an incurable speculator and had, it seems, a special knack for failure. At one time or another he took fliers on timber and mining claims, a steam pulley, a new means of marine telegraphy, an engraving process, an invention that vaguely resembled a television, a self-adjusting vest strap, and the Paige compositor, on which he managed to lose two hundred thousand dollars. His own proclivities probably helped him train a gimlet eye on the spirit of the age, a pervasive gullibility, greediness, and ethical negligence. *The Gilded Age*, written with Warner, was his hilarious send-up of this state of the union, especially the scandal surrounding the Crédit Mobilier and the construction of the Union Pacific Railroad. Not only was it an instant best seller, it went on to become a Broadway smash that then toured the country. The novel's title has remained with us as the apt characterization of the period's essential fakery.

Colonel Sellers is Twain and Warner's memorable creation of an all-American confidence man. The Colonel, an irrepressible optimist and infectiously charming fraud who manages to delude himself even while fooling others, dabbles in speculations of all sorts, land and railroads especially, but always driven by the native instinct for the main chance, the ever-renewable dreamscape of his countrymen. The Colonel (a self-appointed title) combines a capacity for gargantuan exaggeration with a remarkable faith in his most preposterous schemes; he is a catalogue of homespun American foibles. The pure enthusiasm with which he manages to envision luxury amid the most miserable discomfort mirrors perfectly the perverse optimism, the ingenuous zeal, that marked the national character and made it so readily mulcted. Casualties pile up as the novel rolls along. Democracy is disgraced, workers are left unpaid and abandoned to their fate, intimate feelings among lovers, family, and neighbors are prostituted or silenced—all the collateral damage of the confidence man.[13]

■

At no time in the subsequent history of Wall Street did it ever manage to shed the image of the confidence man. But this was emphatically the case during the Crash of '29 and the Great Depression that followed. The impact of those events was so powerful that for a long generation the Street lived in the shadow of a profound distrust. It had earned that obloquy through its assiduous milking of the public confidence all through the boom years of the 1920s.

Jazz Age confidence men came in two flavors. There were men like Charles Ponzi, risen out of social obscurity, light-years removed from the elite, white-shoe world of the Morgans, Belmonts, and Seligmans. A former vegetable dealer and onetime forger and smuggler, forty-two, handsome, and glib, Ponzi made his sensational debut in America just after World War I ended. The scam he invented was stunningly simple. Investors loaned him ten dollars without collateral and he promised to pay back fifteen in ninety days. To the legions who lined up to join his scheme, he explained that he would invest their money in buying up International Post Union reply coupons overseas and redeem them in various markets around the world to take advantage of fluctuations in the value of foreign currencies. Money rolled in at the rate of a million dollars a week. Ponzi bought a controlling interest in the Hanover Trust Company to enhance his liquidity, as well as his legitimacy. He moved into a fancy house and drove around in a flashy "Locomobile." By the early summer of 1920, he was famous. By the end of the summer he was in jail for fraud, where he stayed until 1934, when he departed for Italy and the life of a minor fascist government official. He died a pauper in Rio de Janeiro in 1949.[14]

There were others like Ponzi, also outlanders, though more closely tied to the Street. Ivar Krueger, the "Match King," was the idol of Sweden and the financial savior of a brace of central European nations in the 1920s. He was a titan whose empire stretched around the globe. One country after another granted him a match monopoly in return for life-preserving loans. Krueger and Toll securities traded everywhere. After the crash, however, it all went up in smoke: the Krueger kingdom rested on fraud and deceit—$100 million in forged bonds—not detected by the company's negligent investment bankers from the venerable firm of Lee, Higginson. Ivar Krueger committed suicide in Paris in 1932.[15]

Michael Meehan was an Irish upstart, part of a cadre of ambitious Irish speculators that included "Sell-'em" Ben Smith and Joseph Kennedy. Meehan was a onetime theater-ticket agent who first made an impression securing aisle seats at Broadway hits for his aristocratic Wall Street clientele. Later he struck it rich running an inside trading operation in RCA stock. He carried on his manipulations after the crash, even after the creation of the Securities and Exchange Commission, when he faked insanity to avoid prosecution. But he was eventually expelled from all the exchanges.

And there were notorious lone-wolf speculators like Jesse Livermore, Joseph Kennedy, and others who fit perfectly that frightening specter of those "scoundrel bears" mocked by Melville's riverboat confidence man. Livermore, "the man with the evil eye," was a practicing Calvinist and a lecher who had been around since the war. Supremely vulgar—he called Wall Street a "giant whorehouse" and brokers "pimps"—he was also cagey, superstitious, and a show-off, flaunting his yellow Rolls Royce, steel yacht, and huge sapphire pinky ring. Reduced to penury by 1940, a two-time bankrupt, no longer taken seriously by anyone, Livermore shot himself in the cloakroom of the Sherry Netherlands Hotel. A rambling eight-page suicide note intoned a stark judgment: "My life was a failure." Kennedy, pilloried like Livermore for his vampirelike conspiracies, amazingly enough became the first head of the SEC under Franklin Roosevelt.

Even when these men were riding high in the 1920s, their Wall Street speculations were considered so devious, so premised on creating false illusions among naive investors, that even if strictly speaking what they did was legal, it didn't smell that way. People like Jack Morgan wouldn't deign to do business, much less engage in social intercourse, with men like Kennedy. Yet after the crash it turned out that many of the nation's leading Wall Street bankers were involved in schemes no less unsavory. Investment pools were conspiracies of inside traders designed to pump up the price of a chosen stock. Pool members would then dump it on an unsuspecting public as the price collapsed. Pools were essentially legal conspiracies of market professionals and their privileged clients which manipulated the market through carefully planted rumors and quick, concentrated infusions of cash. These pools were orchestrated by men like William Crapo Durant, the era's most notorious poolmeister and thrice-bankrupted founder of General Motors. Invitations to join a pool were extended to a select circle of financial and political luminaries. Pools like the famous insider group that whipped up enthusiasm for RCA stock in the late 1920s (RCA, the dot.com of its day, rocketed from $85.25 a share in 1928 to $549 in September 1929) were put together by distinguished circles of financiers; in RCA's case, Durant along with Charles Schwab of United States Steel, John Jakob Raskob of DuPont, Walter Chrysler, and Woodrow Wilson's onetime aide and confidant Joseph Tumulty. Often pool organizers were themselves directors of the corporations whose stock they were putting into play, dumping it on the public when the time was ripe. For these select insiders pools were sporting as well as moneymaking affairs, having about them the thrill of hunting to hounds. One observer who tracked their peregrinations talked of "the lure of action, of quick profit, the thrill of battle, the call of the chase, the glamour of admission into a charmed circle, the attraction of mysterious enterprise." Such pools operated in 105 of the 550 stocks listed on the New York Stock Exchange.[16]

After the crash, it turned out that a number of these same eminent men had been involved in tawdry schemes designed to enrich themselves at everyone else's expense. So, for example, Sunshine Charlie Mitchell had lured thousands of National City Bank clients into the most dubious of investments—among them the notorious "Peruvian" bonds and the insupportable loans to the Brazilian state of Minas Gerais that his own analysts had declared destined for default. Even Mitchell's personal financial affairs were a mess. He had skirted the law prohibiting a commercial bank from trading in its own stock and speculated in the stock of his own bank. He had, moreover, concocted a transfer of ownership of stock, at a fire-sale price, to his wife to escape the taxman. Other Wall Street luminaries were similarly compromised.[17]

Most shocking of all was the story of Richard Whitney. If ever one man personified white-shoe Wall Street that man was Whitney, an old-money thoroughbred. From his silver-haired mane to the burnish of his Wetzel suit, he exuded the aura of commanding self-assurance. The scion of a family that arrived on the *Arbella* in 1630, son of a bank president, educated at Groton and Harvard, and polished at the Porceleian Club, Whitney ran his own Wall Street firm. His brother George was a senior Morgan partner. His wife socialized with the Vanderbilts. His father-in-law was a former president of the Union League Club. Richard relaxed at the most recherché country clubs and spent weekends hunting foxes and raising champion Ayrshire cattle on his 500-acre New Jersey estate. Immaculately coiffed, tan, lean, and possessed of an erect gracefulness, Whitney was a specimen of physical perfection as that new Wall Street ideal was stylized by the white Protestant elite.

By the early 1930s, Whitney was president of the NYSE, an exquisite embodiment of its traditional hauteur. He spent the first half of the Depression decade declaiming from on high and denigrating with great regularity every effort of the New Deal administration to reform and regulate the Exchange, proclaiming the purity of the ancient regime with a holier-than-thou éclat. But the self-righteousness and aristocratic bonhomie concealed a shocking secret. Whitney had been for years on a long downslide greased by failed and sometimes whacky speculations and had fallen desperately in debt. As he wore out his welcome, and his last available lines of credit dried up, Whitney resorted to embezzlement and fraud to keep afloat. He even used his position as treasurer to misappropriate funds from the New York Yacht Club, a favorite Brahmin hangout, and stole from the Exchange's gratuity fund. Finally he was discovered, tried, and convicted of embezzlement, all under the hot lights of national notoriety. FDR, who had been a classmate of Whitney's at Groton, registered the global shock: "Not Dick Whitney," the president gasped as the ex-president went off to Sing Sing dressed in his somber black coat and bowler.[18]

Whether men of impeccable credentials or shady characters like Charles Ponzi, these financiers had depended on the complicity of their victims, as is the case with all confidence men. The Roaring Twenties got its name in part because of the mass infatuation with the stock market as a passway to instant wealth. This delirium was fed, as stock market booms tend to be, by an enthusiasm for the era's newest technologies: radio, chemicals, electronics, synthetic textiles, and aeronautics especially. Expectations soon lost touch with reality. Many came to believe that these vanguard inventions and discoveries would transform not only particular industries but the whole way of life in America, or at the very least the nature of the economy. As the decade unfolded, a widespread conviction emerged that the economy had achieved a new plateau of permanent prosperity, that this was a "new era." The old laws of the business cycle, with their exaggerated booms and disastrous busts, had been abolished, so the faithful believed. Speculation had been domesticated, even made scientific by the application of advanced mathematics, its inherent riskiness reduced to a minimum.

These were illusions. To some extent they were perhaps inherent in the uniquely powerful position of the U.S. economy following World War I. In part they grew naturally in the soil of that indigenous optimism and sense of the nation as history's (or God's) chosen land, a transcendent belief that has always seemed an American birthright. And, too, they drew on that instinct Jeremiah Church had early identified as pervasive among his countrymen, that in America "every man is a speculator." But in part these illusions, which in turn pumped up a stupendous overconfidence, were deliberately fostered by those who hoped to take advantage of it. Wall Street financiers and industrialists, distinguished economists, print and radio journalists filled the air with predictions of an endless boom. John J. Raskob, for example, reared in a cold-water Hell's Kitchen tenement but more lately of DuPont and General Motors, as well as head of the Democratic National Committee, raved, "Everybody ought to be rich," in a widely circulated article in the *Ladies' Home Journal.* His plan pivoted around an Equities Securities Company run by a trusted board of directors that would buy common stocks and turn over the profits to average working people. One might invest as little as fifteen dollars a month and, if the dividends were left to accumulate, eighty thousand could be collected in twenty years. The nationally renowned Yale economist Irving Fisher famously prophesied on the eve of the crash that "stock prices have reached what looks like a permanently high plateau." Thomas Lamont of the House of Morgan told newly elected President Herbert Hoover that "the wide distribution of ownership of our great industries should go a long way to solve the problem of social unrest" and that "the future appears brilliant." Just in case there were any Doubting Thomases left, Wall Street operators bribed radio commentators to whip up enthusiasm for their favorite stocks.[19]

For all of this flim-flam and airborne enthusiasm to take root, there needed to be a willing suspension of disbelief on the part of those being conned—what today we might call irrational expectations. And there was plenty of that, ranging from the ridiculous to the sublime. Predicting the market assumed a dozen faddish forms. One "system" foretold bearish downturns in any month containing the letter "r." Another tracked sunspots. Yet another derived its picks from a code assembled from comic book dialogue. Evangeline Adams, a famous fortune-teller, held court in her studio above Carnegie Hall, where she issued a monthly newsletter that explained how shifts in planetary positions were bound to affect the market: "a guaranteed system to beat Wall Street." In *The Great Gatsby* and in short stories like "Paradise Lost," F. Scott Fitzgerald captured the boozy eroticism that implicated Wall Street in the nation's love affair with bootleg gin, jazz, and the "flapper." The Street itself became glamorous and sexy, a site of universal intoxication. Financiers, once depicted as stodgy, obese, and aged, received a makeover in national magazines, reemerging as lean, fashionably dressed, and alluringly youthful. The Street's elders were treated as wise men, accorded the status normally reserved for great philosophers or statesmen. The ignominy that washed over the Street in the aftermath of the crash was as deep and long-lasting as it was just because millions had so recently placed their unreserved confidence in its sagacity. It was reviled not only for its aristocratic arrogance but for its sleaziness and its abuse of the nation's confidence.[20]

■

It could be said that much of what went on in the 1920s repeated itself in the 1990s. This is true, but also not entirely true. Memories of the dot.com bubble, its calamitous bursting, and the cascade of Wall Street and corporate scandals that followed for years in its wake are still all too fresh in the public mind. Once again average folk were swept up in techno-messianism, this time connected to biogenetic and information technologies. (A scientist interviewed in *Forbes* magazine described Interferon—a family of proteins once thought to be a cure for cancer and Wall Street's first wonder drug—as "a substance you rub on stock brokers.") Once again the media jettisoned their native skepticism and contributed to the mass credulity. Just as in the Roaring Twenties the air filled with talk of a new era, justifying stratospheric stock prices for Internet companies that were more virtual than real (often merely the fever dream of some Silicon Valley postgrad) that had not even brought a product to market much less realized a profit. So, for example, the *Wall Street Journal* could gush about the Netscape IPO (initial public offering) that launched the Internet stock bubble: "It took General Dynamics Corporation forty-three years to become a company worth today's $2.7 billion in the stock market. It took Netscape Communications Corporation about a minute." Wall Street media stars like Abby Joseph Cohen of Goldman Sachs issued warnings against what she called FUDD—fear, uncertainty, doubt, despair. After some initial reservations about "irrational exuberance," Alan Greenspan, the chairman of the Federal Reserve Board and the nation's chief economic guru, began issuing blue skies assurances that this new age economy and booming stock market had limitless potential. The "information superhighway" was the twentieth century's fin de siècle version of Melville's "New Jerusalem . . . so called."[21]

Moreover, the ballyhoo bucked up everyone's confidence with the fatuous assurance that confidence games by insiders were a thing of the past thanks precisely to the advent of the World Wide Web, which presumably made information transparent and available to everyone. What had still seemed visionary during Wall Street's Jazz Age season in utopia now appeared imminent; namely, that indeed everyone could safely become a speculator, that Wall Street 'R' Us.

Just as in the 1920s, however, there were confidence men aplenty ready to seize the moment. And once again they came from both the periphery and the pinnacle of society. Young men and women on the make mastered the essential credo of the con game, that appearances are everything. A movie aptly named *Boiler Room* depicted a world of high-pressure, seductive stock promotion and fraud that in its essentials would have seemed familiar to Martin Chuzzlewit. Ambitious young men, trained in emotional thuggery and motivational overkill—they had memorized all of Gordon Gekko's lines from the film *Wall Street*—scam the innocent if covertly covetous citizens of "shareholder nation." The psychic economy had not changed in three-quarters of a century. The head honcho in *Boiler Room* instructs his apprentice con men that above all they must always "act as if . . ." They are Melville's "knaves, wrong-side out" playing upon the malignant innocence of the credulous. And their marks were themselves seduced by the sexiness and adventure of high-risk financial escapades. For day traders and others this world offered a playful escape from the deadening routines of workaday life, a revivifying sneaky thrill whose intensity was accentuated because the stakes were so high.

Some operators went too far, an occupational hazard. Online investing had vastly expanded the capacity to run confidence games en masse. In one case, a pimp whose day job was managing an escort service used his off hours to fleece wire victims. In another, two men running an Internet penny-stock fraud were shot. And in one instance a confidence man from cyberspace found himself hanging by his heels out the ninth floor window of an office building, left there by rival stock promoters.[22]

Since the days of the bucket shop, Wall Street had struggled to distinguish itself from the world of the "boiler room." But as the 1990s wore on that became harder and harder to do. One satiric novel, *Bombardiers* (1995), by Po Bronson, captured the atmosphere of outrageous and cynical hyping of dubious securities by prestigious investment banks and brokerages. This had already become a notorious Wall Street pastime during the Reagan years. The savings and loan industry debacle of the late 1980s smelled fishy enough as Wall Street sucked up the assets of the nation's most prudential and cautious financial institutions, inveigling them into outlandishly risky, even reckless speculations. Michael Milken, indicted on ninety-eight counts of racketeering, fraud, and insider trading; Ivan Boesky, who assured the graduates of Berkeley's business school that "greed is healthy"; and others did time in jail for their more flagrant junk bond deceptions. Drexel Burnham Lambert pled guilty to six felony charges of mail, wire, and securities fraud and paid $600 million in fines, leaving the firm bankrupt by 1990. Michael Lewis's *Liar's Poker* (1989) made fun of the ethos of macho bluffing and sly manipulation that fired up the bond trading departments of houses like Salomon Brothers.

By the mid-1990s, things had gone so far over the top that only satire could penetrate the lunacy. *Bombardiers* is a send-up of the stressed-out world of the Wall Street bond trader. Its characters are ridden with neurotic compulsions. They are almost ludicrously competitive. And they are ready to gull their customers into precarious investments without a scintilla of remorse. They prate about freedom while panting after every disaster as a potential source of booty, and see the government as a gigantic slush fund. For these hyped-up salesmen, "Democracy is an obsolete form of management." The new era is "a propaganda economy, an advice economy, a possibility economy, a rumor economy—an economy of tall tales, fish stories, and oral folklore." But they really outdo themselves and enter fully into the antic utopianism of the moment when they concoct schemes to securitize whole nations, planning to charter the Dominican Republic as a Delaware corporation and auction it off as an IPO, bundling its bad debts to the International Monetary Fund, the World Bank, and the United States together into a corporate shell whose bonds can then be dumped on the unsuspecting public in a kind of "shareholder democracy" and "dollar diplomacy" for the new millennium. The heroes foresee investment banks and military contractors foreclosing on whole countries. "Coyote Jack," head of the sales force, wants to put capitalism to work in the Dominican Republic, "turn it around and then sell it. We'll make a killing. . . . In a few years the world is going to thank us for getting rid of government."[23]

When Enron collapsed at the end of 2001, not long after the stock market bubble burst, even the absurdist shenanigans imagined by Bronson seemed to pale in comparison. With the active connivance of many of the Street's most powerful investment houses, not just Enron but a slew of major corporations—Tyco, WorldCom, Adelphia, Qwest Communications, Arthur Andersen—turned out to be little more than stupendous confidence games designed by top management to defraud the investing public, loot their own company treasuries, bankrupt their employees' pension funds, and rig the market, leaving entire communities prostrate. Analysts from prestigious financial institutions who presumably functioned to supply impartial assessments of company stock instead hyped the securities their firms either already did business with or hoped to do so as underwriters. The complexity and deviousness of the subterfuges deployed by Wall Street firms and their corporate co-conspirators to conceal the machinations at Enron and elsewhere made them worthy successors of Philip Arnold and Silent John Slack. Corporate insiders of the top twenty-five bankrupted companies made off with $3.3 billion in stock sales and bonuses as their firms went belly-up. Until these firms were exposed as frauds, their self-promotion as harbingers of unprecedented economic opportunity, even economic democracy, rivaled anything concocted by Colonel Sellers or Jazz Age enthusiasts of the "new era."[24]

Yet despite the chilling similarities, public reaction to Wall Street's transgressions was more muted than might have been anticipated, especially given the scale of the abuses, their organic connection to the implosion of the stock market, and the fact that they continued to surface with mind-numbing regularity for years after the original Enron scandal. Certainly, compared to the aftermath of the Crash of '29, Wall Street escaped severe censure for its systematic betrayal of public confidence. The sole legislative response, the passage of the Sarbanes-Oxley Bill, only demanded a modicum of new information from the securities industry. Some Wall Street houses were forced to pay substantial fines for their misbehavior, and a number of corporate officers and financial industry executives ended up bankrupt and behind bars. But no one, for example, called for the renewal of the Glass-Steagall Act, the New Deal's principal regulatory protection against the inherent conflict of interest between commercial and investment banking operations housed within the same enterprise. Instead, its repeal in 1998 signaled the ongoing national infatuation with the free market that had taken root in the Reagan years. Nor were there any information-age "money trust" investigations; even the level of moral outrage seemed tepid compared to what had nearly befallen William Duer or the pool-meisters of the 1920s. Indeed, Lewis Lapham, in *Harper's* magazine, characterized the government agenda as an act of "class warfare . . . not the angry poor sacking the mansions of the rich, but the aggrieved rich burning down the huts of the presumptuous and trouble-making poor."[25]

At the outset of his second administration, when new revelations of Wall Street skullduggery were still commanding regular front-page coverage in the nation's metropolitan dailies, President George W. Bush proposed the privatization of Social Security—proposed, that is, entrusting the material well-being of retired Americans to the same financial institutions that had just been found guilty of gross negligence and often criminal misconduct.

The president had mistimed his proposal and overreached himself. The proposal died in Congress, strongly suggesting that the visage of Wall Street as the confidence man still haunted the public imagination. But the fact that the president chose to engage in this battle at what seemed a peculiarly unpropitious moment also suggests something else. Faith in the free market had grown remarkably resilient, so much so that it could tolerate, or at least make allowances for, behavior that would have sparked widespread outrage and calls for decisive action by earlier generations of Americans. Conversely, the public reaction signaled an abiding distrust of government as an economic regulator and protector. There once was a time when citizens mobilized in the political arena to police it and eliminate abuses by private centers of overwhelming economic power. By the turn of the new millennium, however, millions of Americans were persuaded that government bureaucracy inhibited rather than facilitated economic opportunity, democracy, and justice. The kind of democracy many now placed their confidence in might be summarized as "one share, one vote." A great many people had come to think of the market as the medium through which one discovered freedom. Moreover, no major depression followed the meltdown of the dot.com bubble, further diminishing any sense of urgency about mounting a frontal assault on Wall Street's latest reincarnation as the confidence man.

Until such an emergency arises—if it ever does—public alarm and readiness for more drastic measures may remain low. Regardless of whether that proves to be the case, market society will continue to release passions and irrational expectations that Wall Street is bound to exploit. What is noteworthy is how often those who have abused the public trust were at one time or another public heroes of quite an extraordinary sort.

THREE

The Hero

When "the Commodore," Cornelius Vanderbilt, died in 1877, the outpouring of grief was exceeded only by the lavishness with which he was eulogized. Flags flew at half-mast at City Hall, at the Stock Exchange, at Grand Central Station, and along the routes of his railroads. Journalists and politicians hailed him as "one of the kings of the earth" and depicted him as an engineering visionary, a manager of operations so vast and complex they required a kind of military genius to master. One British observer who otherwise viewed the world of Wall Street with bottomless contempt, excepted the Commodore, who "assumes the royal dignity and moral tone of a Gaetulian lion among the hyenas and jackals of the desert." The *New York Herald* summed him up: "It was one honest, sturdy, fearless man against the world, and in the end the man won."[1]

Writing within a few years of Vanderbilt's passing, his first biographer, who considered the Commodore's story a "model for
boys and young men," described his character and accomplishments in terms normally reserved for men of genius, warriors of
extraordinary courage and improbable triumphs, or statesmen of
surpassing wisdom. Without the Commodore, he concluded, "no
railroads or steamships or telegraphs; no cities, no leisure class,
no schools, no colleges, literature, art; in short no civilization."[2]

Vanderbilt had enjoyed this legendary reputation long before
he died. Stories—some true, some half true, some pure fable—
circulated widely celebrating his rough-and-ready vigor and dash,
his commanding presence, his extraordinary valor, his sexual
prowess, and his insouciant irreverence. One such tale depicted
him at the helm of his yacht during a terrifying storm, the ship
floundering, a collision imminent, captaining the boat to safety
while all aboard froze in panic. This tale reeks of mythmaking,
but another comes closer to being genuine, an anecdotal account
of the Commodore's frontier brashness, for which he was sometimes condemned but more often admired. Confronted by a rival
to his Nicaraguan Steamboat Company, Vanderbilt disdained any
resort to the legal system and bluntly told his competitors,
"Gentlemen: You have undertaken to cheat me. I won't sue you
for the law is too slow. I'll ruin you."

This image of the Commodore as a man's man of implacable
force, someone prepared to act outside the law who would brook
no interference with his imperial will, was the stuff of dime nov-

els, penny newspapers, and schoolboy hortatory, but also of more staid editorials in middle-class periodicals. Moreover, it evoked a kind of masculine aggressiveness and sexual potency that added to the Vanderbilt legend. Father of twelve, six feet tall, red-cheeked, with a shock of white hair and flowing sideburns, the Commodore was reported to be a man of gargantuan appetites and especially seductive to women. Whether the latter was true or not—and the evidence suggests it was—the aura of machismo further burnished Vanderbilt's public presence as a hero steeped in the deepest reservoirs of American folklore.

Nor did the Commodore consider mythic self-promotion beneath him. In 1869 he had erected, partly at public expense, a monument to be known as the Vanderbilt Memorial Bronze. It was a stupendous piece of masonry located at the depot of the Hudson River Railroad in Saint John's Park in New York City. The depot itself was nothing short of colossal, an ornate building whose huge pediment was capped by a 12-foot-high statue of Vanderbilt. The Commodore's fur-coated, stony likeness was surrounded by bas-reliefs depicting his fabled career on land and sea. A 50-ton cyclorama included carvings of steamships and locomotives, Neptune and a sea monster, boilers, birds, machinery, cows, pineapples, and railroad tracks. The monument's unveiling unleashed florid Hosannas to the Commodore and his "luminous sagacity." One newspaper noted that while it was perhaps "not so prodigious as the Pyramid of Cheops, nor so lofty as the Colossus of Rhodes . . . it will do."

Public reaction to the Bronze was by no means universally favorable. Some were appalled by its vulgarity, its egocentric hyperbole, and its transparency as a form of self-exculpation. After all, for large numbers of the urban and rural middle and working classes (and, for that matter, Knickerbocker patricians and New England Brahmins), Vanderbilt remained a figure of insatiable greed and lawless deceit, a confidence man writ large and so a moral stench in the nostrils of polite society. A whole generation of his fellow Wall Street Robber Barons—including Russell Sage, Daniel Drew, Jim Fisk, and Jay Gould—suffered the same fate.

Nonetheless, as the Commodore's miraculous elevation suggests, in the years following the Civil War these men managed to shed their less savory associations with the suspect world of the confidence man. Many of their countrymen began to think of them as Napoleonic. This division of opinion reflects the ambivalent sentiments Wall Street has always provoked; indeed, there were plenty of people who were simultaneously awestruck and repelled by what they saw. The *New York Herald*, a paper otherwise critical of the Erie Railroad debacle, nevertheless felt compelled to acknowledge that the schemes devised by Fisk and Gould "exhibit Napoleonic genius." Moreover, it is not incidental but on the contrary essential to their mystique that many of these men began life as men from nowhere. They underwent a transmutation—with some poetic license one might describe an arc stretching from confidence man to colossus—which captured a primal feature of the country's democratic faith.[3]

Napoleon gripped the popular imagination all through the nineteenth century. His legendary status naturally was largely owing to his military genius and imperial omnipotence. But what also counted heavily in the way people reacted to men like Vanderbilt or Fisk was a plebian assertiveness that was also part of the Napoleonic mystique. Their unprepossessing backgrounds, their earthy irreverence toward established ways of doing things or established social authority, their audacity in taking the law into their own hands, their fearless embrace of the risky and the unknown reminded people of the French emperor. Napoleon, that Corsican upstart risen out of social obscurity, was after all a hero of the democratic revolution, his whole life a monument to a supreme act of self-creation. It was in that spirit that these new Wall Street conquistadors were welcomed into the pantheon of native heroes.

"Jubilee Jim" Fisk, for example, presented himself as a living caricature of the conquistador as commoner. His Wall Street wheelings and dealings kept him always one step ahead of officers of the law and placed him perpetually on the precipice of financial disaster; he had an infatuation for risky undertakings, the riskier the better. But the braggadocio with which he carried them off left people gasping. When caught red-handed trying to rig the market for gold, Fisk's aplomb was breathtaking: "Nothing lost save honor," he is reported to have said with a grin meant to provoke. Half the time he dressed like a race-track tout, the rest of the time as a naval admiral, a title he bestowed on himself to go with the captaining of his ocean-going steam yacht. The old Grand Opera House on 27th Street and 8th Avenue where he set up his headquarters—known as "Castle Erie"—was extravagantly remodeled until it looked like a cross between an upscale bordello, a Broadway palace, and a museum of medieval knick-knacks; it included a throne cobbled together with gold-studded nails and represented a kind of corporate Xanadu, gaped at by throngs of passing New Yorkers. There he carried on a flamboyant and adulterous affair with a former showgirl, a scandal he did nothing to conceal from his wife, who remained silently sequestered at home in Boston. Indeed, his sexual passions would prove his untimely undoing when he was murdered by the new lover of his onetime paramour in the lobby of the Grand Central Hotel.

By the time that happened, however, Fisk had already achieved wide popular acclaim as a kind of Wall Street Robin Hood. In part this was thanks to his immediate and generous response to the great cataclysm of the Chicago Fire in 1871 when he commandeered his railroads to rush emergency supplies to the devastated city. A ballad celebrating that feat remained a barroom favorite for many years after Fisk's death. But the reason thousands turned out in New York to mourn his passing and lined the tracks running to his final resting place back home in Vermont had as much to do with his meteoric rise from circus barker to champion Wall Street speculator and railroad impresario, a daredevil trip taken in high hilarity and with a hero's disdain for the conventions that stifled the desires of littler men. He was the Donald Trump of the nineteenth century, a vulgar and vainglorious spectacle, but a man whose ascent excited a sneaky thrill among legions of spectators who secretly wished they could be so bold. Fisk, who had a way with words, put it best: "I was born to be bad," he once said; and who could entirely resist that?[4]

This was a peculiarly American form of cultic idolatry in which men of suspect reputation morphed into heroic scoundrels or heroes of irreverence. The mountebank had become king, but an irregular, eccentric kind of king. Freebooting, skirting the law, or living beyond its reach, this new hero was half warlord, half Everyman, yet, like Napoleon, not altogether either. He was a hybrid character in a raw, hybrid economy, enmeshed in a society obsessed with the infinite possibilities of uninhibited beginnings: a pathfinder and a mogul at one and the same time. With the grime of fishing boats and circuses still clinging to them, these heroes built themselves grandiose palaces staffed by liveried servants and paraded about in the finest European equipages. But they fooled no one. Beneath that gilded veneer they remained the ruffians they started out as . . . and that was a vital part of their heroic charm.

The conjoining of such disparate, even paradoxical, traits created a Wall Street confection (although one by no means confined to Wall Street) that fascinated the generation that straddled the

Civil War. This figure left a legacy that still colors our sense of the Street. "Diamond Jim" Brady, Charles Yerkes, Joseph Kennedy, Michael Milken, and Ivan Boesky all belong to a larger gallery of Wall Street Napoleons stretching from the Gilded Age to the age of the dot.com billionaire. Each in his own way confirms a cultural image of the gunslinger financier: imperious, self-made, ruthlessly ambitious, and full of masculine bravado. They were and still are perceived as outlanders: outside the law, outside established institutions, outside the conventions of normal social behavior. Indeed, it was because they were not to the manor born that their rise and mastery have the romantic aura of democratic adventure, turning roguishness into heroism.

Still, despite this cultural continuity, Wall Street as a theater of the heroic has undergone its own historic makeover. What its protagonists have set out to conquer, what they have risked, how their daredevil doings have affected the rest of us, how Americans have measured their exploits, even the way they have paraded their masculinity, all these and more have registered the profound upheavals over the past century and half in the structure of the economy and the character of American culture.

■

Wall Street's first heroic age coincided with the birth pangs of the country's economic modernization, a ferociously competitive undertaking accompanied by stupendous technological achievements, unimagined changes and improvements in everyday life, and great social suffering.

Conquistadors from the Street had much to conquer, Mother Nature for one, for they were involved in the single most challenging enterprise associated with this formative phase of the Industrial Revolution: the crisscrossing of the continent's vastness with the world's most formidable railroad network. Cornelius Vanderbilt, Jay Cooke, Edward Harriman, James Hill, and even pure speculators like Jim Fisk and Jay Gould were involved, some more intimately than others, in the planning and execution of enormously complex engineering marvels. They needed to know at least something about constructing bridges and tunnels and overpasses, about the complexities of iron and steel rail production, about the vagaries of the weather and the geological eccentricities of largely unexplored terrain. Andrew Carnegie, before he became a steel manufacturer, grew rich selling railroad bonds, not by building railroads. Still, to convince investment houses at home and abroad to buy the securities of new railroad ventures he had to make a persuasive case that the road's planners were capable of hurdling the technological and natural obstacles that stood in their way. For a layman, his knowledge of the arcana of bridge construction, in particular, was impressive.[5]

Subduing mountains and deserts and trackless wilderness was, however, merely the back-story to even more recalcitrant objects of heroic conquest, particularly other men. All these Wall Street champions came equipped with a merciless instinct to dominate that tolerated no resistance, whether from rival speculators or duly constituted public authorities. They seemed promethean figures, indefatigable, and, like frontiersmen, prepared to do what had to be done in the remorseless battle to win out over their opponents.

As their enterprises grew in scope the most intractable center of resistance to their power emerged from among the thousands of skilled and unskilled laborers whose efforts they sought to co-ordinate and exploit. This confrontation was protracted and sometimes bloody. During the Great Railroad Strike of 1877 cities from coast to coast witnessed insurrectionary standoffs be-tween government militias and private bodies of armed men in the employ of the railroad barons on one side and infuriated workers and their sympathetic families and neighbors on the other. During his war to the death against the Knights of Labor striking against his western railroads, Jay Gould, in an outburst of cynicism and Robber Baron braggadocio, threatened that he could hire one half of the working class to kill the other half. Domination of this kind played to mixed reviews, but by the turn of the century most such resistance had been subdued and the mastery of these titans confirmed.

And then there was the marketplace itself, a place so mercurial it eluded every would-be conqueror. Beneath its prosaic exterior of trucking and bartering, the market was a threatening zone of chronic uncertainty, no matter how much people tried to make its workings predictable. This was emphatically the case in late-nineteenth-century laissez-faire America. The market was as free as it ever would be—free certainly of any public supervision and free too of most of the traditional constraints and customary rules that once limited the sovereignty of the law of supply and demand. No one could doubt how fatally dangerous a place the market had become. Beginning in 1837 and continuing until the eve of World War I, panics and depressions erupted with deadly regularity about every fifteen to twenty years. They left in their wake a trail of bankrupted businessmen and speculators (not to mention dispossessed farmers and unemployed workers), irrefutable evidence that such "freedom" bore a heavy price.

Wall Street's heroes took the market's dog-eat-dog imperatives with deadly seriousness and accepted, even welcomed, its amorality. For them the free market was first of all free: that is, a game whose rules were few, fragile, and meant to be bent or broken to conform to the wills of its most implacable players. Their triumphs were therefore enveloped in a romance of industrial privateering, as if they were reincarnations of the English sea dogs of the sixteenth century, living on and crossing the border of state-sanctioned piracy, who synthesized the greed for gold, the appetite for adventure, and the love of exploration into an unquenchable spirit of capitalist enterprise. Starting out with little or nothing, they put together or presided over vast systems of daunting financial, engineering, and logistical complexity. Industries, towns, and cities, entire unsettled regions were given life (or deprived of it) as the hero financiers executed their grand calculations. And even if in the end they were defeated by the market's wildness, they could be admired for their Faustian panache.

Finally, these Wall Street titans had to conquer themselves, perhaps their greatest challenge. Everything they did—or so it seemed to their growing armies of mesmerized spectators—entailed risk. They lived their lives as ongoing encounters with chance, with the hot breath of disaster at their backs. And they never blinked. They remained cool when many lesser men—Wall Street was full of them—panicked. Risk was the arena in which they proved their manhood, in which they created themselves anew, in which they worked their will and exercised their mastery over the natural world, the world of men and machines, and the fickleness of fortune.

An aura surrounded these financial adventurers that had nothing to do with whatever material accomplishments might appear on their résumés. As great speculators they belonged not so much to a profession or occupation as they did to a state of spiritual subversion. They lived in a formless infinity of pure money, a universe with no fixed values, where it was unwise to take anything for granted. If the Wall Street hero might be likened to Napoleon, he was also regarded as kin to the plunger, the wildcatter, the mystic traveler to uncharted and dangerous lands of fathomless risk. It was an exhilarating world, dizzying, and it carried with it the headiness of unadulterated freedom. Those brave enough to expose themselves to its vertiginous atmosphere broke free of the world of work and its strictures of inner moral discipline. They recognized no authority, treated all men with egalitarian indifference, and responded only to the universal mathematics of the disembodied market. In a society that encouraged in every man the dream of one day risking all and breaking free—"self-reliance" as the signature American promise and imperative—the spectacle of Wall Street's champion gamblers walking a tightrope with no net imparted a metaphysical thrill.

One might rightly ask, Why Wall Street especially? To be sure, there were plenty of other Robber Barons, industrialists who kept their distance from Wall Street or even intensely disliked it. Andrew Carnegie was one, although he came to this position only after spending lucrative years as a bond trader dealing with the major American and European investment houses. Henry Ford was another, a man who never got over his primal aversion to financiers. And these men were, like Vanderbilt, Fisk, and Morgan, lionized for their audacity and sangfroid and like them lived under the sign of the Conquistador. But Wall Street's "titans of finance" occupied pride of place. First they were deeply implicated in the era's signature enterprise, railroads, whose capital needs were so enormous they could not get out of the planning stage without huge infusions of money mobilized by Wall Street. That alone left the Street's luminaries in a conspicuously commanding position.

Something more subterranean was at work as well. Wall Street seemed to distill—in the mysteries of its machinations, the exoticism of its specialized vocabulary, the intangibility of what it trucked and bartered, its unpredictability, its penchant for masquerade, intrigue, and dissimulation, its inscrutability, and its capacity to derange the whole economy—the quintessence of risk. If you could master all that you were a hero indeed. The speculative looting and relooting of the Erie Railroad or the bravura attempt by Gould and Fisk to corner the market in gold were appalling and morally outrageous. But they also fascinated the nation because they combined the mastery of an arcane expertise with dauntless bravado and were staged on the edge of a cliff. And their timing was perfect. Just as the western frontier was receding into the past, and with it the proving ground of the frontier hero, that same character seemed to migrate back east to stake out new territory in the financial badlands of Wall Street.

A distinctive vocabulary inscribed these men in the urban-industrial legend. Popular media poured out stories of financial titans whose traits mirrored the technologies they had come to dominate: men of iron with wills of steel, blessed with magnetic personalities and what might be called "titan's eyes," the kind that could look right through you. The most celebrated example of these can be found in Edward Steichen's photograph of J. P. Morgan, which hangs in the Metropolitan Museum of Art in New York. Steichen was so struck by Morgan's eyes that he compared looking into them to staring into the headlights of an oncoming locomotive. Contemporaries, even critical ones, invariably described these men as "bold," and "magnificent of view," "full of verve," capable of absorbing a hard blow without flinching, "audacious," "keen," and possessed of that icy composure that could stand up to the worst possible news. In James D. McCabe's 1870 classic celebration of self-made American heroes, *Great Fortunes and How They Were Made*, portraits of Vanderbilt and Drew pictured them as kingly yet humble, plain but hypnotic, specimens of men whom Shakespeare called "born great." Though the two were different in dozens of ways, one insider nonetheless captured what he saw as their elemental likeness: both "have the mind of crystal, the heart of adamant, the hand of steel, and the will of iron."[6]

Treated as American primitives, these men had a plebian brashness and a virility that observers marked and often envied. This exaggerated sense of masculinity and potency was of a different order from the sexuality of the Wall Street confidence man. If the latter was seductive, he was so in a womanish sort of way: wily and flirtatious, a "girly-man," perhaps, in the eyes of the less enamored. These Gilded Age buccaneers, on the contrary, were Terminators. E. L. Godkin, the founder and editor of *The Nation* and a passionate hater of these Wall Street pirates, was particularly impressed, not in an entirely negative way, by their roughness and size. Fisk dressed "like a bartender, huge in nerve as in bulk"; Drew lied and stole his way to wealth with "tobacco juice drooling from his mouth." August Belmont, who otherwise affected an air of social refinement foreign to ruffians like Drew and Vanderbilt, enjoyed a reputation for sexual allure based as much on his immense financial and political power as on his brooding eyes and dark good looks. So, too, Vanderbilt's feats of physical strength were part of his legend, as was his braving of the British blockade during the War of 1812. Indeed, the personal triumphs of these Wall Street heroes were easily assimilated into the nation's own growing muscularity, its urge to plunge boldly into the unknown and emerge the master, to contend with the great powers of the earth for global supremacy.[7]

Wall Street's heroes helped revise almost beyond recognition an old-fashioned image of middle-class Victorian masculinity identified with thrift, perseverance, responsibility, integrity, chastity, and honesty. Over and over again a set of warrior attributes associated with power, will, and force were singled out for special regard, implicitly demeaning the boring utilitarianism and methodical routine of the reigning version of bourgeois manliness. A river of second-rate novels and magazine short stories circulated this image of the financial tycoon as warrior far and wide. Theodore Dreiser, who was far better than second rate, is especially illuminating in this regard. His reputation as a left-wing writer notwithstanding, the awestruck vantage point from which he viewed the financial titan in his trilogy *The Financier*, *The Titan*, and *The Stoic* make of Dreiser a kind of hostile witness for the prosecution, his work evidence of how compelling the visage of the conquistador had become.

Dreiser was a social Darwinist, though of an aberrant sort. Orthodox social Darwinism, as espoused by William Graham Sumner (the Yale professor who was Herbert Spencer's chief exponent in America) held that "the millionaires are a product of natural selection. . . . It is because they are thus selected that wealth . . . aggregates under their hands. . . . They may be fairly regarded as naturally selected agents for society for certain work. They get high wages and live in luxury, but the bargain is a good one for society." Dreiser, however, did not buy into Sumner's social meliorism or moral theology. He was, rather, a Darwinian fundamentalist. Fitness implied nothing one way or another about social progress or moral order. It was a cold fact of nature, barren of higher meaning, without any redeeming solicitude for the human condition.[8]

The first volume of Dreiser's trilogy opens with a Darwinian epiphany. As a young boy, Frank Algernon Cowperwood, the story's protagonist, makes a life-defining observation. Watching a heavily armored lobster devour a vulnerable squid, young Frank discovers the answer to the question "How is life organized? Things live on each other—that was it," is his spare and unblinking conclusion. That ethos is the thread running through Cowperwood's whole career as a financier, an occupation that in Dreiser's view is neither benign nor demonic. It is predatory, to be sure, but so is all of nature. It can bring calamity, but the universe is not, as the social Darwinists believe, an orderly place but inherently unstable and out of anyone's control: in the narrator's view it is a world of "jungle-like complexity . . . a dark, rank growth of horrific, but avid life—life at the full, life knife in hand, life blazing with courage and dripping at the jaws with hunger."[9]

In the course of the first two volumes of the trilogy, Cowperwood abandons every vestige of sanctified convention. He becomes a living impiety, a defiler of Christian ethics and bourgeois decorum, true only to the parable of the lobster and the squid. He jettisons even a purely rhetorical deference to the ossified maxims of competitive free-market capitalism. He mocks the culture's pious faith in the democratic way, coolly suborning gang-loads of public officials. And his faithlessness is all-embracing. He cheats shamelessly on his wife, Lillian, a priggish, passionless creature of formidable social rectitude. Unlike his peers, whose adulteries and shady business practices are fogged over by pious pretense and feigned shock, Frank does not work to conceal his transgressions. Nor is his adultery a petty fling; it is a grand sexual passion for an indecently young girl, herself a creature of fecund beauty, impulsive, sexually ravenous, and highly dangerous to Frank's fragile social reputation. Indeed, Cowperwood's eroticism is not only as potent as his magnetic attraction to financial empire-building; it is fundamentally the same unquenchable craving for conquest and control. It allows no compromise.

Dreiser is not squeamish about any of this. The trilogy avoids moralizing and harbors no second thoughts. This kind of distanced view, free of irony, is at the core of what Dreiser understands to be happening in a world reconstructed by the great forces gathering around Wall Street. Cowperwood is a mighty player of the game: ruthless, impressively powerful—an exploiter, to be sure, but one whose power to exploit expresses a fundamental law of life; an exploiter who is also a creator of wealth and builder of cities. Cowperwood is a blunt, granitelike figure of considerable density, not easily reducible to the moral polarities of an earlier age. He stands at the heart of an awesome, amoral brute matter-of-factness.

■

J. P. Morgan was in many ways utterly unlike Frank Cowperwood or the real-life financial sea dogs Frank emulated. Unlike many of them, Morgan was an American aristocrat, steeped in the cosmopolitan sophistication of Knickerbocker New York, Brahmin Boston, and Rittenhouse Square Philadelphia, a world seeded with the right clubs, the best schools, and the socially registered. Fisk, Vanderbilt, and Russell Sage excited the public imagination precisely because of their vulgar incivility, irreverence, and appetite for risk. Morgan, on the contrary, was all decorum. Prudential, circumspect, risk averse, well-bred, he was a practicing patrician. The Wall Street that preceded him was renowned for its speculative abandon. Its heroes were gamblers, lone desperados stalking the financial badlands. They were in the American grain. Morgan stood outside it. He hated speculation. He hated the free market. Yet for those very un-American attributes and attitudes he was looked up to by millions of his fellow citizens. He was a Wall Street hero of a new type. Dreiser might have recognized his special "fitness" for the latest stage in the economy's evolution, which seemed to demand a kind of Olympian dirigisme.

When he died in 1913 Morgan was eulogized extravagantly, in part for qualities he seemed to share with his predecessors: a certain ruthlessness, huge ambition, self-assurance, and of course those tycoon eyes. But most of all what comes across is the sense of Morgan as a savior. When the tales of his legendary business deals had been recounted—of his preeminence among his fellow investment bankers, his philanthropic generosity, his breathtaking collection of art and antiquities, his confidential relations with presidents, kings, and prime ministers the world over—something quieter, less visible, but of even greater gravitas resounded. Morgan had instilled order and integrity, or so his admirers were convinced, on an economy that seemed dangerously without them. The nation's preeminent banker had managed to "bestride the world like a Colossus" not because he dominated the stock market; that was too superficial a view. He was a preternatural financier for whom the ticker tape recorded not dollars won and lost, but a "panorama of rushing trains and roaring factories." Financial operations that when performed by lesser men might leave one queasy were cleansed of improprieties in his hands. "Character First Was His Philosophy," declared a *New York Times* headline. *Harper's* lapidary encomium anointed him a "matchless upbuilder of properties . . . a faithful trustee of billions, full of faith in his country and his fellow man. . . . Above all a true patriot." He was, in a word, the nation's savior.[10]

Chaos is the dark side of the free market. Never was that more true than during the last third of the nineteenth century. The fin-de-siècle economy was characterized by internecine competition and insecurity, punctuated by periodic panics and two severe depressions, one in 1873 and another twenty years later, each of which took years to lift. The urban working classes and family farmers suffered the worst. But small- and middle-sized businessmen as well as middle-class professionals and a growing population of white-collar workers were hit as well. This intermittent derangement of the economy had profound social and political consequences. Relations between the rich and poor grew more brittle and explosive. The Populist Party threatened to bring those social animosities into the political arena. Many saw the election of 1896, in which the Democratic candidate William Jennings Bryan condemned the Republicans and their Wall Street controllers for crucifying mankind on a "cross of gold," as a day of reckoning. A foreboding that the nation might, once again and not even a generation removed from the Civil War, be dividing in two gripped the popular imagination. More than any other figure from the world of business, J. P. Morgan seemed to offer hope, a presence commanding enough to restore order.

Three moments in particular illuminate how the country's most esteemed investment banker earned his reputation as a heroic savior. The business of railroading was Exhibit A to the growing multitudes convinced that the free market simply didn't work. The record of senseless overbuilding and duplication of lines, of overcapitalized, watered stock, of dangerously rotting rails and capital-starved equipment, of gross corruption and incestuous relations between railroad financiers and the construction companies hired to build the roads was more than infuriating. It was suicidal. Each new panic was prompted by a railroad bankruptcy that, during the era's more serious depressions, set off an avalanche of others. More roads defaulted during the depression of the 1890s than at any other time in American history.[11]

Beginning in the 1880s, the House of Morgan initiated a series of interventions which resulted in the reorganization of the country's railroad network. What today might be called financial reengineering established a discipline through centralized management overseen by Morgan and a small coterie of white-shoe investment bankers and lawyers. Lines were merged, water wrung out of bloated railroad securities, slash-and-burn competition inhibited. The new regime eliminated the worst of the old abuses. Railroads remained objects of speculation and insider deal making. But these innovations in corporate architecture, widely known as "morganization," which frowned on speculation and the free-for-all irrationality of the free market, imposed law and order. For this Morgan earned the sobriquet "Bismarck of the railroads."[12]

What Morgan achieved with the railroads was a prelude to his even more far-reaching structural overhaul of the whole economy. During a few short years, from 1897 through 1903, together with a select circle of Wall Street investment bankers, he invented the publicly traded corporation which we now take for granted as the basic organizational form of economic life. These men did not actually invent the modern corporation, but they did foster and finance a great merger movement in these years that produced such household names as General Electric, International Harvester, and, most famous of all, United States Steel, the world's first billion-dollar corporation. A century of economic free-for-all vanished in a decade. Between 1895 and 1904, 1,800 firms were swallowed up in corporate mergers. The 1900 census recorded 73 industrial combinations valued at more than $10 million; ten years earlier there had been none. By 1909, a mere 1 percent of all industrial firms accounted for 44 percent of the value of all manufactured goods. The hundred largest industrial corporations quadrupled in size. In 1909, 5 percent of all manufacturing firms employed 62 percent of all wage earners.[13]

This intense reshuffling of the economic order eliminated a mass of heretofore privately owned, fiercely competitive companies across a broad range of industries. In their place "peak" corporations, underwritten and overseen by Wall Street's elite financiers—Kidder Peabody, Lee, Higginson, the Belmont interests, Seligman Brothers—along with the largest commercial banks, such as Chase National Bank, National City Bank, and First National Bank, established their dominance. They rationed out supplies of scarce capital and undertook to reorganize the

core of the nation's productive apparatus. Morgan and his colleagues installed a new kind of managerial cadre who came
equipped to run the sophisticated, centralized, and specialized
bureaucracies erected to ensure the durability of these colossal
corporate combinations. This new managerial trusteeship, while
mindful of its obligations to stockholders and the bottom line,
was also charged with guaranteeing stability and good order
within the corporation and in its relations with the outside world.

By 1903, the merger movement had revolutionized the economy. A genteel clubbiness dampened the impact of competitive
rivalries; they lived on, but under watchful eyes. For many who
had grown weary of the free market's chaotic uncertainty and de-
structiveness, its chronic cycles of overproduction followed by
mass shutdowns and bankruptcies, the new order, even if less
free, was a godsend, an act of salvation whose architect deserved
the highest praise.

But the American economy was big and getting bigger. Like
any vigorous capitalist economy it continued to inspire new
entrepreneurial energies, technological breakthroughs, competitive upstarts, and speculative risk taking. The reach of J. P. Morgan, impressive as it was, could not encompass everything, nor
was this Wall Street world, including Morgan himself, immune
to tempting but shaky speculations and potentially ruinous con-
tests for financial supremacy. Panics, still part of the market's ge-
netic makeup, lay in wait.

One erupted in 1907 with near-catastrophic consequences

when a major trust company failed, threatening to bring down the whole financial edifice with it. This turned out to be the third and definitive step in Morgan's apotheosis. To this day the story of the financial panic of that year is retold every time there is a major blowup on Wall Street. The melodrama of Morgan's heroism runs invariably like this: Those were the days when a single man held the fate of the nation in his hands. Morgan acted with courage, decisiveness, and cool deliberation when all around him, dignified bankers and brokers, were frozen with fear, paralyzed into fatal inaction, or caught up in a cowardly race to protect themselves, no matter the consequences. If Morgan had not intervened to quarantine the rapidly spreading contagion, had he not by the force of his personality and his enormous moral capital as the country's trusted, if unofficial, central banker compelled his fellow financiers to pony up the necessary funds to save key tottering institutions, there is little doubt the country would have suffered a severe and protracted crash, a crash, indeed, not confined to America, for the Tokyo and London markets plummeted at the news from New York. His heroics were evidence of his extraordinary power and his just as extraordinary selfless deployment of that power. He was a government unto himself acting on behalf of everybody. Bernard Berenson, the renowned art critic and Morgan's chief adviser in the amassing of the world's most impressive private art collection, struck a note of exaltation: "Morgan should be represented as buttressing up the tottering fabric of finance the way Giotto painted St. Francis holding up the falling Church on his shoulder." Dissenting views—that the great banker might have personally profited, that indeed he might have provoked the panic as a means to other mercenary ends—were dismissed as calumnies. During a time when the authority of public institutions remained severely restricted, especially when it came to policing the economy, when government bureaucracies were limited in reach, staffed by amateurs, and kept on short rations, Wall Street's elite banking fraternity, Morgan first of all, offered to substitute themselves as responsible guardians of the public trust.[14]

So it was that during the age of Morgan, which ran roughly from the depression of 1893 to the Great Crash of 1929, the Wall Street hero took on a new set of traits. Wisdom, expertise, restraint, and disinterested supervision on the public's behalf were grafted onto earlier qualities of command and fearlessness. The Street's performance during World War I, when it became not only banker for America's mobilization but financier of the whole Allied war effort, further burnished its reputation for financial patriotism.

After all, the world war reversed the historic relationship between Europe and America, one in which the latter had always played the role of the dependent partner. This dependency was resented by millions of Americans. Not only was it painfully felt by American bankers; it had seeped down into the lower depths of the Populist Party and its outcry against the "English devilfish." Every new war loan to the Allies was a nail in the coffin of that "enslavement." In four years the United States went from being a leading debtor nation to the world's chief creditor. Overnight the country liquidated its age-old debt to Europe. Meanwhile, rivers of capital from all over the world flowed into New York, the only place it could safely pool without fear of depreciation. In this atmosphere any opposition to Wall Street's role in the conduct of the war did not so much vanish as drown in a tidal wave of martial enthusiasm.[15]

Above all, the bravery of the "Silk Stocking Regiment" confirmed the Street's new reputation for financial knight errantry. The 107th Infantry regiment, made up mainly of Society boys from Manhattan (along with a sprinkling of upstate "apple knockers"), took on the impregnable Hindenburg Line (known in Germany as the Siegfried Line), a formidable zigzagging series of stony fortresses interlaced with underground tunnels, like something out of *The Lord of the Rings*—just as lethal, just as invincible—in the fall of 1918. The regiment was badly mauled. It suffered the highest single-day casualty rate for a regiment in U.S. history. In the process it earned itself a sacred place in the nation's conscience. What a turnabout. Once maligned as a coddled and cowardly collection of class snobs whose only previous distinction was its deployment putting down risings of the lower orders, the regiment found redemption when it punctured the Hindenburg Line. Six months after the armistice, an immense crowd gathered along 5th Avenue—drawn from as far away as Connecticut and Pennsylvania—to welcome these heroes home:

"Welcome home Seventh," they cheered the bloodied and be-medalled Silk Stocking Regiment, Wall Street's knights.[16]

■

Mythmaking about Wall Street's heroic presence began in the Gilded Age and has been with us ever since. It has always rested first of all on a belief that an elect subspecies of men are endowed with a certain genius for triumphing over risk. This has been emphatically the case more recently. One need only recall the Reagan era and the years since then. Think of names like "Chain-saw" Al Dunlap, the asset stripper from Sunbeam, "Neutron" Jack Welch of General Electric, and the corps of samurai-like practitioners of the art of "lean and mean" management, cru-saders on behalf of "shareholder value." For a decade and more their ferociousness and implacability were applauded on maga-zine covers, in best-selling biographies and autobiographies, in gossip columns, and on a slew of new cable television shows catering to the popular fascination with Wall Street as a combat zone. Or recall books like *The Predators' Ball* (1989), which re-counts the high-risk financial acrobatics of Michael Milken and his coterie of junk bond speculators. In fact, the very sobriquet "Predators' Ball" was not, as one might assume, the brainstorm of some publisher's marketing department. It was conceived by Milken and his colleagues to capture the brazen spirit of the an-nual Beverly Hills orgy celebrating their ruthless makeover and dismantling of the country's most formidable corporations. And of course who can forget Gordon Gekko, the cinematic apotheosis of people like Milken and Ivan Boesky? Gekko's infamous but charismatic pronouncement in the film *Wall Street* that "greed is good" both scandalized and seduced. How reminiscent of the way Vanderbilt, Drew, and Fisk had flouted Victorian pieties a century earlier, earning themselves censure but also the awe reserved only for the most daring.

Beginning with the merger and acquisition mania of the mid-1980s, the media were overrun with depictions of Wall Street "gunslingers," "white knights" and "black knights," "killer bees," "hired guns," "shotgun" corporate matings, and " barbarians at the gates," warrior appellations borrowed helter-skelter from antiquity, the Middle Ages, and America's mythologized West. New magazines like *Manhattan Inc.*, *Venture*, and *Success*, as well as established venues like the *New Yorker*, became awestruck documentarians of the era's power-suited corsairs, with their manly horseplay and their O.K. Corral financial staredowns and shoot-'em-ups. Portraits of the biggest deal makers on the Street such as the lawyers at the leading merger and acquisition firm (Skadden, Arps, Slate, Meaghen, and Flam) marveled at their all-around fitness and their regimen of physical workouts, which prepared them for "all-nighters." These were financial athletes at the peak of their game, in it not for the money but for the je ne sais quoi that always seems present at the heart of all true sportsmen, men like the "Liquidator," Asher Edelman, who confided to an interviewer his "Nietzschean desire for control." Bond traders made out like professional hit men and boasted of "ripping the faces off" their clients, while the more cerebral samurai of the financial wars carried around copies of *The Art of War* by Sun Tzu, the Chinese Clausewitz. One young trader caught up in the throes of a superheated deal was overheard exclaiming: "I love it. It's just like combat. It's the real thing." A magazine anointed Michael Milken "Michael the Magnificent."[17]

Remarkably, for the first time in nearly a century scholars began revising the shadier history of the founding generation of Robber Barons. New studies of Jay Gould, J. P. Morgan, and Edward Harriman reconceived them as master builders. This historical revisionism did more than simply revive the Gilded Age hagiographies and the fawning magazine literature of the turn of the century. In these revisionist biographies the well-publicized faults of the old tycoonery were duly noted; in fact, they were reconceived as the natural, necessary, inevitable, and even heroic traits of a bumptious country feeling its oats, preparing to burst onto the world stage as a new colossus.[18]

Soon enough, all these goings-on became commonly referred to as America's second Gilded Age. It was a characterization that would last well beyond the Reagan era, into the dot.com mania of the next decade. Echoes of the present in the past—and conversely the past making itself heard in the present—suggest deep-running similarities between the two Gilded Ages. Like Drew, Fisk, and Gould, many of the Wall Street heroes of the 1980s, including Carl Icahn, Bruce Wasserstein, Saul Steinberg, Ivan Boesky, and Michael Milken, hailed from unimposing social backgrounds, middle- and lower-middle-class outer boroughs and suburbs, and state colleges or no colleges rather than the Ivy League. Their rise out of social obscurity struck a chord, making them living confirmations of that primal national faith that for those with the gumption anything was possible in America. Awe, mixed with envy for those who have ascended from nowhere into the empyrean heights, is an indigenous American cultural instinct. First noted by Alexis de Tocqueville in his portrait of antebellum America, it has remained potent ever since. This emotional chemistry provides the combustible raw material of endless melodramas depicting the rise and equally delicious fall of great Wall Street tycoons and their empires: thus Reagan-era best-sellers included *Greed and Glory on Wall Street: The Fall of the House of Lehman, Barbarians at the Gate,* and *The Serpent on the Rock.*

Like their forebears of the first Gilded Age, the Street's newest breed of financial bad-asses burst on the scene as rebels against the ancien régime, only more so. Michael Milken's "social revolution" aimed at overturning the Street's historic hierarchy. The firm he worked for, Drexel Burnham Lambert, had been distinctly minor league; now it, and a handful of other new arrivals like Kohlberg, Kravis, Roberts & Company, were cock of the walk. "Relationship banking," that genteel world enclosed within mahogany walls hung with Old Masters where "relationships" were premised as much on family and social ties as on mere moneymaking, gave way to, was run over by, "transactional banking." Here every new deal was open to negotiation, each a new test for some Wall Street financial house to prove its commercial bona fides all over again. Milken believed in and milked his reputation as a warrior against the "corporacracy." Nasty microclass struggles for control took place between languorous Ivy League patricians turned out in rimless glasses and the omnipresent breast-pocket hanky and shirt-sleeved, uncouth cigar-chomping geeks from the trading floor staring out at the world through thick-framed black glasses. This too gave a sense of freedom, of fresh blood being pumped through the aerated arteries of an aging financial organism. The rebels' bloody assaults on the corporate and financial bastions of the old order earned them points for fearlessness. And their nerdy outfits gave them extra credit for their social irreverence, a kind of bourgeois version of épater le bourgeois, like the tobacco juice drooling out of Unc'l Dan'l Drew's mouth.

Michael Milken's Aladdin-like junk bond buy-outs, megamergers, and acquisitions formed the vanguard of this upheaval, making him the Lenin of the social revolution. Reared in California, supremely arrogant, and notably modest in what he drove, wore, and lived in, he was perhaps oddly suited to the role of the iconoclastic gate-crasher. He exerted a mesmerizing influence, a charisma that had limousines lining up on Rodeo Drive at four in the morning to do deals, their owners convinced, as one of his admirers gushed, that "Michael is the most important individual who has lived in this century." Why not? In just a half dozen years, 215 industrial and financial companies issued $20 billion in junk bond debt (roughly 13 percent of the total corporate bond market). Household names of the American economy—TWA, Gulf Oil, Walt Disney—were suddenly in play. Three thousand mergers worth $200 billion took place in 1985 alone.[19]

It was an odd anti-elitist revolution, organized from on high and exuding a messianic aura. As a "social revolution" it was designed to save America from itself, from its fat-cat complacency. Stripped of poorly performing assets, malingering workers and their feather-bedding unions, doddering and absentee managers, and intrusive government bureaucrats, American business would rise again. Only men who had themselves risen from social obscurity could appreciate and meet the challenge. Companies languishing in commercial oblivion, financially distressed but with untapped potential, could be resurrected, but it would take the audaciousness of a new financial knighthood.

In these same ways, however, Wall Street heroes of the second Gilded Age were quite unlike the model epitomized by J. P. Morgan. When the captains of industry and finance lorded it over the country at the turn of the twentieth century, no one would have dreamed of calling them rebels against either an overweening government bureaucracy or an entrenched set of interests. There was no government bureaucracy to speak of to rebel against, and these men were themselves "the interests," Wall Street chief among them. People like Morgan, Andrew Mellon, and Henry Clay Frick worried about being overthrown, not about over-throwing someone else. A Gilded Age peopled by irreverent, leo-nine youngsters out to shake up the old order has a distinctly different feel from one run by lugubrious, bearded patriarchs whose very physical heft cried out their sense of entitlement and rever-ence for good order.

Just as Morgan's emergence as a new kind of Wall Street hero signaled a profound shift in the underlying structure of the political economy at the turn of the century, so too did the rise of Wall Street's rebels during the Reagan years highlight another fateful turning point. However, it was a more dubious one. Wall Street "heroism" during the closing decades of the nineteenth century, no matter how much it transgressed law and morality, was bound up in the vast transcontinental industrial explosion of the country. Wall Street heroes had their hand in all the nation's great undertakings— coast-to-coast railroads, gigantic steel, oil, and raw materials industries, pioneering technologies in electricity and chemicals, the dazzling cornucopia of new material delights. Moreover, these stupendous feats of production and innovation drove the economy.

A hundred years later, however, Wall Street stood at the center of a decaying productive apparatus. The billions of dollars trad-ing hands during the Reagan (or Milken) era measured what one commentator aptly called the "financialization" of the economy. It concealed an underlying stagnation: the 1980s were marked by a relative lack of investment in new plants and machinery, bare-bones budgets for research and development, and the contraction or folding up of precisely those core industries that were the hallmarks of the first Gilded Age. Instead the economy relied on the heady vapors given off by the financial services sector. Wall Street became a revolving door for the exchange and re-exchange of nominal assets; corporations buying other corporations; public companies taking on freight loads of debt to go private; privately held firms auditioning for their debuts on the public equities market; a kind of "paper entrepreneurialism." Between 1979 and 1990 the proportion of total private investment in plant and equipment that went into the financial, insurance, and real estate sector (FIRE) doubled. And between 1984 and 1990, one-quarter of all private investment ended up there.[20]

Our most recent cult of the titan, the maestro of risk, emerged amid a mood and even the reality of national decline. It followed the defeat in Vietnam, the scuttling of the postwar financial system inscribed at Bretton Woods, the rise of OPEC, "stagflation," the wholesale deindustrialization of the country's midsection, an inferiority complex regarding the Japanese economy, the humiliation of the Iran hostage crisis, and more. How unlike the environment of late-nineteenth-century America, when the country was clearly on the rise, an awakening giant flexing its muscles.

Does the heroic stature of Wall Street diminish under such

circumstances? Does it matter that once the lions of the Street were identified with great material accomplishments but that more recently, especially during the fabled 1980s, their names have been linked to the economy's dematerialization? Perhaps this can account for what might be characterized as the declension of the masculine mystique long identified with the titan of finance, indeed, even its faintly comic or comic-book inversion. During the Reagan era the country was introduced to the "big swinging dick" phenomenon made famous by *Liar's Poker.* This was the easily satirized world of Gordon Gekko or Larry "the Liquidator" (from the play and film *Other People's Money*), an adolescent male fantasy world of "rip their eyes out" raw bravado and violence. The Wall Street "hero" of Tom Wolfe's *Bonfire of the Vanities* is a "master of the universe" not because he is one— on the contrary, he is a quivering mass of insecurities, duplicities, and fears—but because he has borrowed the name of one of his six-year-old daughter's favorite over-muscled superhero toys. All this preening and chest-thumping might have struck their titanic forebears as unnecessary or even demeaning. One senses here an instinct for revenge and overcompensation gestating during the years of national frustration and decline.

Early on the Wall Street hero was given life by his association with the country's mighty material explosiveness; later, by living off its financial fall-out. In either case, however, the Street has always seemed to thrive thanks to somebody else's efforts. From the time of Jefferson through to the present, Wall Street has appeared to many people under the guise of the parasite. And for our ancestors especially the parasite was more than a species of economic deadwood. First and foremost the Wall Street parasite was a sinner.

FOUR

The Immoralist

Henry Ford was an American folk hero. He was singularly identified with the country's favorite new technology, the automobile. But it was his character, even more than his inventive or organizational genius, that most endeared him to his fellow countrymen. Ford seemed a living embodiment of virtues considered quintessentially American and responsible for the nation's extraordinary good fortune. He hailed from small-town, rural America, where hard work, frugality, modesty in dress and deportment, a practical-minded affinity for the mechanical arts, piety, and self-reliance were first nourished and still commanded respect. Ford never strayed far from those roots; indeed, as his legend grew, publicists deliberately exaggerated his rural origins, burnishing his reputation as a twentieth-century version of the Jeffersonian yeoman. He neither drank nor smoked, and long after he became an industrial tycoon, he was still showing up for work at dawn. By the 1920s, Ford was so widely esteemed he was semi-seriously considered presidential timber, running well ahead of President Warren G. Harding in the polls.

So it was not a complete shock that when he published a dyspeptic tirade against an alleged conspiracy of international Jewish financiers it became a best seller. Appearing first in 1920–21 as a series of articles in a newspaper, *The Dearborn Independent*, that Ford controlled, the pieces were subsequently gathered together as a book under the inflammatory title *The International Jew*. There had always been a tincture of the conspiratorial in the country's anxiety about the intimidating power of finance, Wall Street in particular. And anti-Semitism had always been an ingredient in that phobic fantasy. This went at least as far back as the days when Wall Street banker August Belmont, representative of the Rothschilds in the United States since the panic of 1837, became the object of vicious Jew-baiting during the Civil War. The *New York Times*, for example, had this to say about Belmont, then chairman of the Democratic Party: "The notorious undenied leader of the Democratic Party at Chicago was the agent of the Rothschilds. Yes, the Democratic Party has fallen so low it has to seek a leader in the agent of foreign Jewish bankers."[1]

Ford, however, raised the stakes considerably in his journalistic scapegoating of a Jewish Wall Street, lending an extraordinary ecumenical reach to an ancient prejudice. For the automaker, a secret cabal of international financiers was responsible not only for

the subordination and parasitical leeching away of life-giving industry and agriculture, not only for the bloodbath of World War I,
not only—wondrously zany as it might seem—for the Bolshevik
Revolution but also for the rank impiety that he saw sweeping like
a contagion across postwar America. What Ford was most exercised
about was the perilous state of precisely that world of small-town,
Protestant, abstemious, proudly independent, and hard-working
America: he saw a way of life that once ruled the land and for
which he had become a cherished emblem in danger of vanishing.

The International Jew explained how this state of affairs had
come to pass. It discovered the hidden hand of Jewish financiers
behind virtually every form of urban, cosmopolitan popular
culture—the pornography, oversexed novels, and titillating magazine illustrations of the publishing industry; a movie business
given over to glamorizing promiscuity and the high life; big-
time gambling, including the "Black Sox" World Series scandal
of 1919; bootleg liquor; "Jewish" jazz; Broadway degeneracy;
and a half-dozen other symptoms of moral decline that Ford
associated with the city and its infatuation with consumer culture. Wall Street, in Ford's view, was the incubator of a mod-
ernist debauch, feeding the nation a steady diet of cheap thrills
and sexual innuendo.[2]

Henry Ford's historical reputation comes down to us largely
airbrushed clean of this crackpot nastiness. And it is true that
after the public outcry against *The International Jew* became so
clamorous and widespread that his own car dealers were up in

arms (once business began to suffer), Ford was compelled to apologize. Nonetheless, the fact that the book did so well suggests a strong undercurrent of sympathy not only for Ford's anti-Semitism but also for his apprehension of Wall Street as the fount of a pervasive hedonism which threatened the moral integrity of American society.

Wackiest of all was the auto tycoon's bizarre notion that bankers and Bolsheviks were in league to undermine capitalism and the bedrock middle-class morality upon which it rested. Yet this weird formulation was also the most telling. For people who believed as Ford did—and there were millions of Americans who did—capitalism was as much a moral order as it was an economic system for producing goods and services. The capital accumulator was a virtuous person not because he was rich; he was rich because he was virtuous. His distinctive virtues were familiar to every American schoolboy: he depended only on himself, worked hard and saved for the future, resisted the temptation to indulge in frivolous pleasures of the moment, and honored honest labor and its material accomplishments, all to achieve a self-mastery that would keep him safe from the snares and delusions of a sinful world.

Bolsheviks believed in none of this. To begin with, of course, they proclaimed their intention to abolish private property, the ground on which the character armor of the capital accumulator was forged. The Bolshevik threat was more global, however, more than a mere challenge to the prevailing system of political economy. It promised to do away with a whole set of vital institutions,

beliefs, and customary ways of behaving: the church, the patriarchal family, monogamy, individualism, and patriotism. Together
they made up the moral edifice of capitalist civilization; without
them that civilization was inconceivable, and one was left staring
into the abyss of moral chaos. At least, that was the grim and pan-
icky premonition that darkened the national mood in the years
immediately following the Russian Revolution and World War I.

But what did Bolshevism have to do with Wall Street, international finance, and the Jews? Wall Street, after all, was the
quintessential capitalist institution. Or was it? Insofar as it lubri-
cated the mechanisms of trade and investment, yes it was. But as
a cultivator of the moral virtues Ford and many others prized it
inspired grave doubts.

Money made on the Street, many were convinced, was not the
product of hard work, nor, more often than not, was it made
honestly. What it "produced" was intangible, ephemeral as paper,
and socially useless. Indeed, like a parasite it leeched away real
wealth that originated elsewhere. Parasitism, in this view, was as
much a moral indictment as it was an economic category. Wall
Street bred attitudes and behaviors that seemed demonically designed to undermine the very capitalist superstructure it was
supposed to support. The Street encouraged an addictive fond-
ness for gambling and the desire for easy money. Like a casino
it preyed on human frailties, in particular the yen for a life of
pleasure-seeking idleness. It rewarded trickery and deceit rather
than the straightforward, transparent dealings the marketplace

was presumably based on. Prices for what it traded shifted from day to day, sometimes from minute to minute, without any apparent rhyme or reason, subverting values fixed for generations, placing a premium on cynicism, even toward the hallowed institutions of hearth and homeland. The Street's single-minded pursuit of money without regard for its source or purpose nourished an all-consuming selfishness.

So too, Mammon worship, whose altar was the Stock Exchange, was a stateless religion. Like Bolshevism it recognized no loyalties to God or nation. Jewish bankers leagued with Jewish Bolsheviks were inherently subversive. Ford even concocted stories about circles of Jewish financiers secretly plotting with the Industrial Workers of the World and the Socialist Party to make war on the world of gentile capitalism. Because international financiers dealt in monetary abstractions, unmoored from their local origins in particular workplaces, families, regions, and countries, their allegiances could not be trusted. Ford's anti-Semitism was rooted in that lack of trust. For centuries Jews had been ostracized in just this way: as a stateless tribe of parasitical and merciless Shylocks. Despised by every nation, they felt loyalty to none. Once confined to the margins of the capitalist marketplace, now, according to this updated version of anti-Semitism, they occupied its inner sanctums. Capitalism had been Judaized; once a haven of Christian rectitude, now it was a playground for the anti-Christ.

In the eyes of Ford and other critics, Wall Street poisoned the moral atmosphere. How could the fear of God, or bedrock beliefs in frugality or self-restraint, or respect for diligence and perseverance, or devoted service to family and nation survive in it? Moreover, Wall Street's insidious penetration of the new avenues of popular entertainment and communications worked to spread the decadence. Consumer culture thrived on the same narcissism, self-absorption, insatiable desire for immediate gratification, and flight from the discipline of work and its libidinal inhibitions that once seemed peculiar to Wall Street and less legitimate forms of moneymaking. Consumerism transgressed every boundary—religious conviction, ethnic solidarity, patriarchal authority, social hierarchy—that might get in the way of the desiring, self-seeking individual. It propagated a rootless cosmopolitanism that undermined all established channels of moral legitimacy. Primordial capitalism, the kind Ford stood up for, had been evangelized by the new capitalism, the capitalism of mass consumption, the devil's capitalism, the Jewish capitalism that had always been Wall Street's secret desire.

Ford was caught in an irony of his own making. No product was more closely identified with consumer capitalism than the automobile, and no man was more responsible for its universality than Henry Ford. The marketplace obeyed its own logic, however, and made the car a vessel of its maker's cultural undoing. Ford had always hated Wall Street, resented its power, and resisted turning to the investment houses for credit and capital. His animus against the Street was shared by a sizable segment of the business community, especially in middle American midsize cities and towns, where the family-owned manufacturing enterprise was a point d'honneur as much as the source of patrilineal continuity. For a long century Wall Street had been confined to a moral gulag that worked to conceal the spiritual intercourse between industry and finance. But now the Street had escaped the gulag, and people like Henry Ford were frightened.

∎

Wall Street's reputation as a sinkhole of immorality goes back to the earliest days of the republic. Jefferson once described New York as "a cloacina of all the depravities of human nature." He was thinking first of all about Wall Street.[3]

Jeffersonians were preoccupied with the dangers of aristocracy. What they feared was both political reaction and moral decline; or, rather, they were convinced that the political well-being of the new republic depended on its moral good health; if one were endangered so must be the other. Aristocracy fused political subversion to moral corruption. Aristocrats were counter-revolutionaries who wanted to overthrow the new republic and might succeed in their aim because their way of life promised to eat away at the moral fiber of the new nation. Aristocrats, in the Jeffersonian view, were immoralists by their very nature. Their attachment to a life of luxury, their exemption from hard labor, and their gratuitous sense of entitlement were profoundly corrupting. They bred habits of sloth and contempt for all those

Spartan virtues—simplicity, modesty, frugality, independence, honest labor, and meritocracy—without which the whole democratic experiment was a lost cause. Jefferson's profile of the aristocrat expunged all the more admirable features of the aristocratic personality—a sense of honor, courage, disinterested public service, social generosity, and noblesse oblige—which champions of more elitist social and political arrangements like Hamilton naturally emphasized.

In the New World the roots of aristocracy were shallow; that was America's great good fortune and promise for the future. Compared to the Old World, the new country was largely free of titled wealth and hereditary privilege. But a vigilant republic still had to stand guard. Especially in those new sectors of the economy subject to the power of money, great fortunes, accumulated without apparent effort, invited all the moral pitfalls traditionally associated with aristocratic decadence.

"Moneycrats" were singled out as agents of moral disarmament. Their sins were numerous, but three especially seemed most dangerous: those who spent their days trading and speculating in the mystifying value of paper wealth were gamblers, parasites, and hedonists.

Gambling, a habit long associated with the aristocracy (as well as the demoralized lower orders), was considered a religious offense of the first order. In colonial days the Puritan divine Cotton Mather scathingly observed that "gains of money or estate by games, be the games what they will, are a sinful violation of

the laws of honesty and industry which God has given us."
Gambling was considered a form of divination, a devilish practice that presumed on God's prerogative to see into the future.
Speculative trading in the prospective value of land, goods, or
money (or, as in William Duer's case, government bonds) was
merely a modern form of gambling and incited the same hubris
as its older counterparts. Moreover, the gambler shared some
fatal moral disabilities with the parasite and the hedonist.[4]

By the time of the American Revolution there was already a
robust plebian resentment of the aristocrat as parasite, a privileged nonproducer living off the hard labor of those he lorded
over. While once labor carried with it the curse of Cain, in the
new age of the democratic revolution this common fate, to live
by the sweat of one's brow, had found its redemption—indeed,
was sanctified. And suddenly, those, like the aristocrat, the
gambler, and the speculator, who lived off the honest earnings of
others were offensive in the eyes of God. So, too, it was plain to
see that a life free of toil was an incitement to hedonistic revel-
ing. "Stock-jobbing" and "speculations" were part of a whole
Olympics of economic games playing that encouraged libidinal
excess, a dangerous release of animal passions pandering to men's
baser desires. The same plebian tradition that condemned the
aristocrat as a parasite depicted him as congenitally debauched.
How could he be otherwise, lacking the self-restraint that a regimen of hard work imposed? No less than the landed aristocrat of
old, whose limitless appetites for carnal pleasures of the most de-

praved sort were legendary, the moneycrat of the new order was seen as a champion of self-indulgence, chasing after the same evanescent excitements, making a mockery of the moral order.

During the 1790s, when the passions dividing the followers of Hamilton and Jefferson were most inflamed, political broadsides, editorial admonitions, church homiletics, and didactic novels and poems tirelessly condemned these moral failings of the new moneyed aristocracy. One patriotic but gloomy poet worried:

We thought when once our liberty was gain'd,
And Peace had spread its influence thro' the land,
That Learning soon would raise its cheerful head,
And arts on arts would joyfully succeed;
Till all Columbia's genius 'gain to blaze,
And in true science more than rival's Greece;
But Speculation, like a baleful pest,
Has pour'd his dire contagion in the breast;
That monster that would ev'rything devour."

In the popular novel *Dorval; or, The Speculator* the villainous speculator is a moral as well as an economic seducer, a man with a liquid identity, so depraved he even turns his romantic adventures into clever financial ruses. Anti-Federalist ministers sermonized that "barefaced" speculation would undermine "common honesty." Jefferson warned George Washington that moneyed aristocrats were corroding the moral behavior of the new nation, luring people away from industrious labor "to occupy themselves and their capitals in a species of gambling destructive of morality . . . which introduced its poison into government itself."[5]

This Jeffersonian persuasion remained alive and well throughout the nineteenth century. In antebellum America exposing Wall Street's' aristocratic depravity excited the popular imagination, especially during the "age of the common man," when Andrew Jackson became a folk hero. Young women were warned away from romantic attachments to Wall Street brokers, whose trade made them experts at dissimulation and betrayal. John Pintard, a Knickerbocker grandee, cautioned his daughter about such bon vivants, who were bound to end their days in ruin or even suicide. It was telling that some of the city's earliest gambling parlors sprang up in and around the Street and depended on the patronage of speculators whose day jobs were scarcely different from what went on behind closed doors at night. Indeed, an infamous murder case suggested far worse. In 1836 a prostitute, Helen Jewett, was brutally murdered by Richard P. Robinson, a young clerk from the mercantile district. The world he and his pals worked in supported a male subculture whose attitudes about sex, work, and leisure defied the middle-class sense of propriety, including sexual propriety. Cheered on by his fellow clerks, Robinson was acquitted, an instance of upper-class immunity to the law which infuriated less-privileged members of the population, already convinced that Lower Manhattan was a sinkhole of iniquity.[6]

Potboiler novels and journalistic exposés circulated lurid depictions of the Street as a site of lost innocence. Like the ancient sirens of mythology, the financial district enticed callow young men from the countryside to abandon their devotion to work and family and addicted them to a life of compulsive gambling and pleasure-seeking at the cost of everything they once held dear. *Frank Leslie's Illustrated Newspaper*, one of the first to cater to the tastes of the new urban middle class, ran a cartoon depicting the whole fraternity of Wall Street brokers and bankers as a band of inebriates reeling down the Street, empty liquor bottles labeled "bull" and "bear" left in their wake. "Story papers" like the *New York Ledger* that circulated widely among the working classes editorialized in favor of combined moral and economic regulation, calling for enforcement of laws against gambling, defamation of character, and conspiracy to defraud. Over and over again magazine and newspaper illustrations sketched the consequences of addictive speculation: a man, still young but dissipated, lies on a bed, either dying or dead, an empty liquor bottle on the floor beside him, his distraught wife weeping forlornly in the foreground (perhaps a sad small child in the background), with a caption drawing the all-too-obvious moral of the story. *The Adventures of Harry Franco: A Tale of the Great Panic*, was America's first depression melodrama, published soon after the panic of 1837. Harry, its ingenuous hero from the countryside, is mulcted not once but multiple times by unscrupulous commercial hucksters, just in

case anyone might miss the point about the moral perils await-
ing those foolish enough to venture into this secretive world of
treacherous double-dealings.[7]

George Foster, the widely read antebellum pamphleteer and
journalist who combined moralizing with a knack for vivid observation of everyday life in the new and mysterious big city, best
captured this sense of Wall Street as a moral snake pit. In his *New
York by Gaslight*, a series of newspaper sketches of his wanderings,
he described Wall Street as a dehumanizing place: "Wall Street!
Who shall fathom the depth and rottenness of thy mysteries?
Has Gorgon passed them through thy winding labyrinths, turning
with his smile everything to stone—hearts as well as houses?"[8]

This shadowy world, Foster and others suggested, was also
prone to wanton sexuality and sexual perversion. The hedonism
encouraged by a life of fast money and idle hours was bound to
break down inhibitions in all realms, including the sexual. Foster
frightened—and titillated—his readers with images of "milk-
white virgin bosoms given to the polluting touch of lust." Aristocratic presumptions that had grown up in conjunction with mountains of unearned paper wealth encouraged their owners to believe
they could possess whatever they fancied. *The Quaker City; or,
The Monks of Monk Hall* (1844), the best-selling novel of the
nineteenth century until the publication of *Uncle Tom's Cabin*,
was set in Philadelphia's financial center—Chestnut Street was
then more imposing than Wall Street—and vividly expressed this
melodramatic dread of illicit intercourse between aristocratic fi-

nancial power and sexual transgression. Its author, George Lippard, was a widely read journalist, freethinker, and social reformer. His story was erotic throughout and designed to reveal the moral underside of capitalism and the social derangement it fostered. Lippard undressed every "pillar of society," bankers and merchants especially, who spent their days and nights carrying on at Monk Hall, committing repulsive sins—rape and incest among others—in a labyrinthine hideaway well stocked with opium, choice liqueurs, and ruined young women.[9]

Moral anxieties agitated the political realm. President Jackson's enormous popularity had something to do with the way he channeled his constituents' queasiness about the ethics of their commercial zeal. He enhanced his reputation as a hero of the common man by making war against "the Monster Bank," the Second Bank of the United States. The bank was headquartered in Philadelphia and presided over by Nicholas Biddle, a blue-blooded Philadelphia gentleman of surpassing arrogance and thus a perfect foil for Old Hickory's denunciation of the bank as an incubator of aristocratic privilege. Presidential jeremiads directed at Biddle and the bank emphasized the institution's economic immorality. Thundering that he wished "stock-jobbers, brokers, and gamblers . . . were all swept from the land," Jackson warned that "the people of this country shall yet be punished for their idolatry." This indictment was particularly wounding during a time when Americans were taking special pride in their industrious settling and building up of a country that not long previously had been a forested wilderness. It was maddening to watch merchant bankers and speculators heap up unimagined wealth without producing anything tangibly useful. On the contrary, their splendid carriages, Italianate mansions, and liveried help seemed too much like the products of legalized thievery. Moreover, their parasitism and immodest love of luxury were demoralizing, subverting the new nation's commitment to frugal self-reliance. The opulence of financiers served as a moral stigma. But in a country in which pursuit of the main chance was practically universal, it was an ironic one.[10]

Great wealth posed a dilemma. Americans were, after all, in love with moneymaking. Yet they also were deeply troubled by how it was made and what it might bring in its wake. During the antebellum years the issue simmered in the background while the country was preoccupied with the overriding question of slavery. After the Civil War, however, the conundrum of wealth and poverty in the rapidly industrializing economy commanded everyone's attention. And in a debate that ranged from the pulpit to the Broadway theater, Wall Street came to occupy a distinctive niche within the American psyche.

■

America's Gilded Age got its name, in part, thanks to spectacularly ostentatious displays of wealth by a nouveau-riche class of financiers and industrialists. Their extravagance was especially noisome because it coincided with a time of urban and rural squalor, poverty, and desperation so immense that no one in the New World had seen anything like it before. Could it be that the two phenomena were related? Was it possible that the stupendous wealth, which presumably embodied scientific, technical, and organizational progress, was also responsible for poverty, with its calamitous social chaos and moral decline? Did those select few who managed to accumulate such extraordinary riches do so by playing fast and loose with the ethical norms that presumably governed respectable society? If so were they endangering the spiritual well-being of the country? Should they be held to account? Could it be that the amassing of wealth automatically placed the ambitious individual and even the whole of society in moral jeopardy? In the Gilded Age, these questions became unavoidable.

Jay Gould's career captured perfectly the era's moral forebodings. Gould was immensely powerful and controlled some of the country's strategic means of transportation and communication, including the Missouri Pacific Railroad, Western Union, and important metropolitan newspapers. He was a consummate Wall Street speculator, renowned for his cold-blooded ruthlessness. And during his lifetime he was the most hated man in America. Indeed, in the century since his death, and despite history's notorious fickleness, Jay Gould's reputation has remained irredeemably dark. A recent biography of "the Mephistopheles of Wall Street" (the first I know of to attempt his rehabilitation) takes a perverse pleasure in reviewing this unblemished record of moral censure.

Alexander Dana Noyes, the dean of turn-of-the-century financial journalism, judged him a "destroyer." Gustavus Myers, whose *History of the Great American Fortunes* was a seminal work of pre–World War I Progressive-era muckraking literature, called him a "pitiless human carnivore, glutting on the blood of his numberless victims . . . an incarnate fiend." Matthew Josephson's celebrated exposé, *The Robber Barons*, written during the Great Depression, depicted Gould as eerily nonhuman: "No human instinct of justice or patriotism or pity caused him to deceive himself or waver . . . from the steadfast pursuit of strategic power and liquid assets." A biographer writing in the 1960s declared Gould's life "the ultimate perversion of the Alger legend," and an eminent historian of the same period judged that Gould's career "encompassed almost every known variety of chicanery."[11]

Even when he died in 1892 no one could think of a kind word to say. For the editors of the *New York World* he was the "incarnation of cupidity and sordidness." Lamenting the demoralized state of the country's spiritual life, its prostration before "the golden calf," the paper blamed Gould particularly. His success encouraged this idolatry. It "dazzled and deluded multitudes of young men. Jails, insane asylums, and almshouses all over the land are peopled with those who aspired to wealth by similar methods." Moreover, these incarcerated few could scarcely take the measure of this moral plague that had infected many, many more, still "at large, mingling with the community in all walks of life, excusing, practicing, and disseminating the vices of which he was the most conspicuous model in modern times."[12]

Silent and secretive, Gould nonetheless lived his life inside a luridly lit bubble of public infamy, a purgatory of shame. Joseph Pulitzer pronounced him "one of the most sinister figures that have ever flitted, bat-like, across the vision of the American people." The *New York Times* was scandalized and despaired for the cause of civic virtue so long as "the insidious poison of an influence like that of Jay Gould can be detected . . . and when people claiming to be respectable are not ashamed of being associated with such a man as he." Even his sometime partner in financial skullduggery, James R. Keene, whose own slyness earned him the sobriquet of Wall Street's "Silver Fox," judged Gould "the worst man on earth since the beginning of the Christian era."[13]

Jay Gould was the original Wall Street immoralist. Condemnations this extreme suggest that he had become something more than a human being: he had achieved the status of a metaphor, a vivid piece of iconography in the folklore of a genteel culture wrestling with the paradoxes of raw industrial capitalism. Gould stood as a living insult to all the Victorian pieties and sentimental illusions that polite society found so necessary to veil its own mercenary ardor. The Mephistopheles of Wall Street fascinated not because he was unique but rather because he seemed to distill in his person and career a set of character traits and behaviors commonly associated with Wall Street that the world of bourgeois, middle-class propriety found deeply detestable.

Wealth, even the accumulation of great fortunes, did not by itself offend the cannons of respectability. Tooth-and-claw, give-no-quarter combat in the competitive marketplace was also acceptable, even a point of manly pride . . . so long as it was conducted according to the implicit ground rules of Protestant morality. But Wall Street, and not just in the person of Jay Gould, seemed always to be testing, and often transgressing, those ground rules. The nub of the problem was that despite the growing cross-fertilization of the Street and the new industrial order (especially the railroads), the two had not yet mated or produced offspring. Manufacturing, distributing, and selling the products of American industry and agriculture were carried on, in the main, by small- and medium-size family firms and partnerships. Under normal circumstances, these had no intercourse with Wall Street. But Wall Street banks, brokerages, and free-lance speculators lived off the abnormal cyclical crises endemic to this nineteenth-century family capitalism. Victims of these crises suddenly discovered that their fate was more closely bound up with the Street than they wished or had realized. Naturally they treated Wall Street as a special kind of incubus.

When it came to pondering the relationship between wealth and work, genteel culture knew certain truths to be self-evident. Work was good, wealth incidental. Work encouraged self-discipline, probity, and good order. Wealth was the tangible outcome of this earnestness. Its accumulation was a perpetual tutorial in self-mastery. Property arising out of work provided the material haven sheltering the patriarchal family. Inside that fortress of land, home, and heritable assets, sentimental affections and the moral education of the young would flourish. In this worldview, property was more than a mass of congealed labor; it was a living, breathing alter ego, a vehicle of self-expression, a passway to creative energies, a proving ground of middle-class manhood, and a moral legacy. Nonetheless, for property to fulfill these functions, for wealth to be legitimate, it had to be accumulated through transparent fair dealing, however tough-minded.

In this way respectable society surrounded its preoccupation with work and wealth with a halo of religiosity, worthy intentions, and rules of correct behavior. Everyone recognized that wealth, however beneficent, was also dangerous. It could be flaunted, but that was a sign of hubris. Wealth could feed an insatiable inner greediness, turning self-creation into self-indulgence. Wealth might lure one down the paths of dishonesty, even if the transgressions were not punishable by law. Wealth might be acquired in what Christian civilization had for centuries censured as the "Jewish way," that is, undeservedly, by leeching away the fruits of the honest labor of others. Wealth might emerge out of dark conspiracies rather than through open transactions. Wealth, like a loaded firearm discharged thoughtlessly or with malice, could wound or annihilate the innocent. During the Gilded Age, when middle-class folk as well as the genteel upper classes turned their gaze to Wall Street they were apt to see overweening pride, ostentation, lack of discipline, wanton idleness, selfishness, dishonesty, parasitism, stealth, callousness—a veritable thesaurus of moral depravity.

Many sorts of people, often with nothing else in common, shared these feelings about the Street. Upper-crust socialites in Boston, New York, Philadelphia, and other colonial-era seaboard cities felt their social and political preeminence threatened by the rise of the nouveaux riches. They were not so much disturbed by the Street's violation of the work ethic—after all, work did not count for much in their own calculus of ethical worthiness—but rather resented the way pure money was storming the barricades of their cherished social exclusivity, based as it supposedly was on nonmonetary values: breeding, education, and cultural savoir faire.

Work-a-day middle-class folk harbored different concerns. They were committed to the moral rigors of work and hostile, not just politically but in their souls, to distinctions of social class. If High Society was offended aesthetically and found chasing after money unseemly, the upright middle classes of town and country considered Wall Street an impiety. The "genteel tradition" which encoded middle-class values as a set of Protestant strictures about work and self-discipline viewed fast money, lavish display of money, money cut loose from its ethical moorings—the sort of money tidal-waving its way through Wall Street—as far worse than unseemly. What went on in Wall Street was an inversion of the moral calisthenics of the work ethic, an indolent lusting after money for its own sake.

Moreover, the Street's imposing power over the two most vital organs of the nation's economic life—credit and the railroads—incited feelings of frustrating dependency among farmers, businessmen, and others that were easily translated into expressions of moral high dudgeon. Such power seemed undeserved, deriving as much from shady dealings, usurious finance, and merciless exploitation of the labor of others as it did from the laying of track, the building of drawbridges, or the choreography of freight trains. A sizable quotient of this high-mindedness no doubt amounted to so much pious cant and unctuous hypocrisy; these same commercially minded middle-class folk might themselves be caught dabbling in the market or engaged in their own cutthroat business practices. But this world of savage incivility, quintessentially represented by Wall Street, genuinely offended their most precious conceits.

Remnants of the country's preindustrial ruling elite, people like the Adams cousins, Henry and Charles Francis, or the British émigré E. L. Godkin (founder and editor of *The Nation*), were lavish in their contempt for the barbarism of the nouveaux riches, especially those whose fortunes came out of Wall Street. The heroine of Henry Adams's novel *Democracy* (1880), Mrs. Lightfoot Lee, the widow of a wealthy financier, expresses her disdain for Gilded Age millionaires who couldn't think of anything better to do with their money than pile it up and flaunt it:

"To let it accumulate was to own one's failure; Mrs. Lee's great grievance was that it did accumulate, without changing or improving the quality of its owners."[14]

Chapters of Erie, the stunning exposé of Wall Street shenanigans in the late 1860s, co-written by Charles Francis and Henry Adams, mainly unmasked the era's rampant political corruption and crony capitalism. But it was impossible to separate the Adamses' political indictment of the Street from their ethical revulsion. The spectacle of financial chicanery they presented damned a whole culture, one that could no longer tell the difference between piracy and legitimate business, that bestowed honors and titles and welcomed into fashionable resorts men "without character" like Gould, Fisk, Vanderbilt, and Drew. Dishonorable men like Drew struck at the foundations of society and were "the common enemy of every man, woman, and child." The Crédit Mobilier debacle, in particular, in which railroad operators connived with government officials to loot the public treasury, persuaded Henry Adams that "the moral law has expired—like the Constitution." Writing about "black Friday"—the newspapers' name for the gold panic of 1869—Adams excoriated Fisk for his "singular depravity."[15]

As the century drew to a close Adams's moral revulsion soured into anti-Semitism. He was tormented by an overwhelming foreboding of the advent of a "Jewish Age," which he gloomily concluded was bound to put an end to everything he cherished (foreshadowings of Henry Ford). Henry and his brother Brooks mourned the imminent demise of those sanctuaries of civilization that were undergoing terminal ecological damage in places like Washington Square, Beacon Hill, and Rittenhouse Square. In the immediate aftermath of the 1893 depression Henry bitterly confided to his brother that he was looking forward to the smash-up of his whole world with a kind of ghoulish glee: "I shall be glad to see the whole thing utterly destroyed and wiped away. . . . In a society of Jews and brokers, a world made-up of maniacs wild for gold, I have no place." The brothers' Judeophobia led them to blame Wall Street for all the social decay, rampant vice, and mean-spirited avarice that was exterminating whatever remained of the self-conscious modesty, refinement, and moral high-mindedness of the world in which they and people like them had grown up. Henry was fatalistic: "We're in the hands of the Jews. They can do what they please with our values. . . . Westward the course of Jewry takes its way."[16]

Brooks was a crankier and more eccentric version of his brother. He not only agreed with Henry, he transmuted Henry's drear premonitions into a general theory of historical decline in his magnum opus, *The Law of Civilization and Decay* (1896). The money power, Wall Street, Jewry—they were synonymous in his eyes—had eaten away at the chivalrous imagination and heroism of the Middle Ages. All residues of an honorable patrician noblesse were corrupted beyond saving. He summed up his bilious conclusion for Henry: "I tell you Rome was a blessed garden of paradise beside the rotten, unsexed, swindling, lying Jews, represented by J. P. Morgan and the gang who have been manipulating our country for the last four years."[17]

E. L. Godkin, who shared the Adamses' distress over parvenu money lust (if not their sulfuric anti-Semitism), used his magazine to excoriate people like Fisk, Vanderbilt, and Gould. Godkin felt at home in Society and was more than a bit of a snob who frowned on the vulgarity of the new plutocracy. At the unveiling of the Vanderbilt Memorial Bronze he let loose a torrent of invective that implicitly condemned the moral bankruptcy of a culture that admired rather than stigmatized Vanderbilt. "Kings of the Street" like Vanderbilt displayed "unmitigated selfishness"; it was appalling, as were their "audacity, push, unscrupulousness, and brazen disregard of others' rights." When Fisk died sensationally (murdered by his former mistress's new lover), Godkin's only regret was that he should have died "in old clothes and in penury and neglect" rather than decked out in "velvet and diamonds" surrounded by fawning reporters. Godkin was deeply suspicious of the rough-and-tumble of democratic politics. Although active in elite circles of government reform, he remained dour about the prospects of raising the general level of public morality. It might be the only remedy for the baleful influence of people like Fisk and Vanderbilt, but he was not counting on it. "People are eager for money and as unscrupulous about the means for getting it."[18]

Acidic denunciations like these of the country's commercial zealotry rang with Götterdämmerung finality. Social elitists despaired for the country's cultural and moral well-being, believed its decadence was possibly irreversible and part of the general decline of Western civilization. They came to this gloomy conclusion out of a historical world-weariness, secular in spirit, rather than from the standpoint of a wounded Christian conscience. Others, however, from less prepossessing social backgrounds burned with the wrath of God.

Religious leaders and their communicants were of two minds. Plenty of ministers from mainstream Protestant denominations felt entirely comfortable providing divine sanction for the accumulation of wealth, blessing a practice their middle-class congregants pursued with ardor. Russell Conwell's sermon "Acres of Diamonds" was the best-known of such justifications. Conwell was a farm boy from Massachusetts turned Baptist minister, and the founder of Temple University, which he envisioned as an institution of educational and moral uplift for the children of the working classes. His homily, first delivered in 1889 and repeated six thousand times over the next quarter century, made the case that not only was the opportunity to make a fortune open to all but that striving to do so encouraged, like regular exercise, the muscular development of strong character. Moreover, some of Wall Street's titans, including J. P. Morgan, were conspicuously pious and contributed heavily to church philanthropies (after all, even the wily and notoriously unscrupulous Daniel Drew founded a theological seminary in his own name).[19]

Still, what went on in Wall Street was disquieting even to the most orthodox clerics. Henry Ward Beecher was by any measure the most widely listened to preacher in mid-nineteenth-century America. He presided over a substantial upper-middle-class congregation in Brooklyn, and his words of moral instruction did not often venture far beyond the horizon of conventional bourgeois belief. But even he rose to rhetorical heights of Old Testament fire and brimstone when it came to issuing judgments about the moral turpitude of Wall Street's bad boys and the plutocracy of which they were a part. Thus Fisk's raffish disregard for propriety infuriated Beecher, who denounced him as "that supreme mountebank of fortune . . . absolutely devoid of moral sense as the desert of Sahara is of grass." When the "Admiral" died, Beecher sent him on his way with an unforgiving eulogy, dismissing him as a "shameless, vicious criminal, abominable in his lusts." Foretelling Gould's demise as well, he described the financier as "a great epitomized, circulating hell on earth"; "when he dies hell will groan—one more woe." Beecher's parishioners, however complacent, nonetheless did harbor doubts about the cupidity and corner-cutting behavior they saw around them. Luxury, conspicuous waste, preoccupation with fashion left them vaguely anxious. Beecher mirrored their misgivings about those who were too eager to pile up possessions, who abandoned their responsibilities as stewards of wealth. They were, in Beecher's view, guilty souls and carriers of moral anarchy. Wealth accumulated unjustly was "a canker, a rust, a fire, a curse."[20]

Other voices were bolder, readier to raise the possibility that the Street itself, not just its most notorious mountebanks, was by its very nature always verging on or falling into sin. The Social Gospel movement offered a general indictment of free-market capitalism as unchristian in its callous disregard for human welfare. In the year of the Haymarket bombing (1886) one of the movement's principal founders, Washington Gladdens, issued a widely read homiletic entitled "The Three Dangers: Moral Aspects of Social Questions," which took on Wall Street directly. Gambling, according to Gladdens, was the worst of the three dangers (the other two were drinking and family disintegration). By gambling he mainly meant speculation, not cards or dice playing. "Speculating in margins" was "immeasurably worse" than ordinary gambling because it was more dishonest. The big-time speculator, the minister observed, "may be a pillar in the church; he may hob-knob with college presidents, and sit on commencement platforms . . . but he is a plunderer." Frustrated by the remarkable deference, even admiration, shown for such people, he for one would challenge the inertia and passivity of the pulpit and work to extirpate the "evil genius of our civilization."[21]

Theological censure and pronouncements from the pulpit were formal expressions of a much more widely diffused and religiously inflected culture. The attacks might be likened to a system of spiritual respiration that naturally expelled a certain kind of economic behavior as a noxious threat to moral health. Gilded Age editorial writers and political stump speakers tirelessly condemned the Street's immorality. Great cartoonists like Thomas

Nast, whose relentless, mocking depictions of the New York's notorious Boss Tweed and his gang of corruptionists led to their overthrow, often drew Wall Street villains resembling reptilian or prehensile devils. Nast sketched gothic nightmares of Wall Street's bottomless depravity. In one, "This Street Is Closed for Repairs," Boss Tweed is caught in prison garb with a ball and chain around his neck walking down Wall Street past a storefront labeled "Cuthem-Cheatem, & Co Bankers," musing as he strolls, "Why a fellow feels quite Honest in this neighborhood." Even popular board games of the period carried the stamp of moral disapproval. One, "The Checkered Game of Life," inscribed its squares with landmarks of moral backsliding and dishonor, including "Gambling to Ruin," "Idleness to Disgrace," and "Influence to Fat Office."[22]

So, too, the literary landscape was littered with didactic novels, plays, and short stories (often serialized in popular magazines aimed at the genteel middle classes in town and country) that worked to affirm Victorian ethics by playing up their violation at the hands of those infected with the Wall Street contagion. Much of this was second-rate melodrama, and to modern ears it sounds intolerably preachy. *Honest John Vane*, for example, a successful moral pot-boiler of the 1870s first serialized in *The Atlantic*, described New York as the epitome of materialistic decay and treated its nouveaux riches as "half Carthaginians and half Sybarites." The story was an allegory, a *Pilgrim's Progress* in reverse. Its hero, "Honest John Vane," once a maker of iceboxes, falls from a state of decency and diligent effort to moral destruction, driven by the temptations of easy money. A smash hit on Broadway, *The Henrietta* (1887), applied the strictest Victorian ethical code to Wall Street and found it in flagrant violation. The playwright, Bronson Howard, frankly voiced his contempt: "I tell you Wall Street represents the fiercest kind of gambling in the world . . . a thousand times deadlier than Monte Carlo." And this is what the play harped on: the way the Street's poisonous atmosphere sickens and kills even the most intimate human affections between father and son.[23]

Some literature achieved more penetrating and convincing levels of moral scrutiny. William Dean Howells's *Hazard of New Fortunes* (1890) captured the anxiety felt by many in the middle classes about Wall Street's insidious undermining of right thinking and right behavior. For all the characters in Howells's novel the consequences of the Wall Street contagion are disastrous, but most of all for Jacob Dryfoos, the patriarch whose tragic undoing originates in his seduction by the phantasms of Wall Street. Dryfoos starts out as an exemplar of bourgeois rectitude, narrow-minded and provincial to be sure, but a true believer in and practitioner of sober-minded, methodical labor and thrifty provision for the future, a forbidding but devoted father and husband, a man possessed of solid moral convictions, "crude but genuine." But then fate, or rather Fortuna, changes everything. Once a farmer, he is drawn away, not without earnest resistance, by the lure of rich neighborhood land and oil prospects. He changes, becomes a kind of vampire, sucking the poetry out of life. Here is Howells's autopsy of the moral cancer metastasizing out of Wall Street into the heart of Jacob Dryfoos as he is forced to confront the true "hazard of new fortunes": Jacob "came where he could watch his money breed more money and bring greater increase of its kind in an hour of luck than the toil of hundreds of men could earn in a year. He called it speculation, stock, the Street." Here Jacob suffered "an atrophy of the generous instincts," here "where he broke down and cried for the hard-working wholesome life he had lost. He was near the end of this season of despair, but he was also near the end of whatever was best in himself."[24]

Howells's high moral seriousness reflected a deep-running cultural queasiness about capitalism run amok. An embedded religious consciousness formed a moral boundary that the Gilded Age sensibility might cross again and again but never entirely efface. Wall Street functioned as Protestantism's moral gulag, an underzone of spiritual undesirables. In this way the Street's rise inspired a kind of counterculture that aspired not to overthrow the inhibitions of an older moral order but to restore them. So pervasive was this Protestant counterreformation that it supplied much of the psychic energy driving the great oppositional political movements of the Gilded Age, including Populism, the antitrust movement, and the Knights of Labor. The platforms and programs of these movements were in no way backward-looking;

on the contrary they anticipated the fundamental reforms of the twentieth century with respect to government regulation of the economy, the rights of labor, and social welfare. But they were grounded in a vision as old as the Revolution, one that yoked labor and virtue like body and soul. By severing the link between wealth and productive labor the Street threatened a devastating spiritual amputation. Legions of angry farmers and laborers and midsize businessmen warned that Americans needed to be vigilant. And their cry for moral vigilance echoed in the anathemas they hurled at the Street.

Wall Street spread an antique nightscape before the populist imagination. It was inhabited by the oversexed and the emasculated, by urban tricksters and sybarites, by moral prostitutes and apocalyptic demons. It was a despoiled landscape, robbed of its natural vigor and hard-earned virtue. Folk poets often rhymed about effete Anglophiles and demoralized fops. Trusts were invariably depicted as tentacled creatures, beasts of vaguely biblical provenance. Vulpine shylocks perched amid "Envy and Pride and Lust and Greed," sequestered themselves in "marble grottos" or "great mausoleums of greed."[25]

The Street's corrupting influence on sexual mores and family integrity was especially alarming. The *Sioux Falls Daily Argus*, for example, singled out for censure Morgan's contribution to "the blighting of womanhood," and "the premature aging of children." Irate farmers raised the specter of "Debased Manhood." Moreover, the fear of emasculation was coupled with an intuition that the extraordinary power wielded by financial overlords bred insatiable and conscienceless lust. The "Oligarchy" ravaged every outpost of female virtue. For populists and many other political insurgents the Money Power was also an impiety and a pollutant that threatened above all the purity of the land, the family, the nation, and the race. A generation before Henry Ford's anti-Semitic tirade, the car manufacturer's darkest phobias about the moral subversiveness of finance capitalism circulated widely through the country's hinterland.[26]

How quaint this all seems now. Our own "second Gilded Age," beginning during the Reagan era, coincided with the efflorescence of fundamentalist and other forms of religious rebirth. Yet modern-day evangelicals pay precious little attention to problems of wealth and poverty or to the peculiar role of the Street in that relationship. If today there is such a thing as basic middle-class morality, it no longer finds moral discomfort in the presence of moneymaking for its own sake. Certainly the old taboos against gambling are gone. However censorious the religious right waxes, it rarely finds a link between the moral looseness it excoriates and the culture of devil may care so flagrantly practiced on Wall Street during the junk bond mania of Michael Milken's 1980s or the dot.com hysteria of the next decade. So, too, this revamping of the nation's religious subconscious has left its impact on the literary imagination. It has blunted the sting and eased the moral anxiety once aroused by such Gilded Age classics as *A Hazard of New Fortunes* and Edith Wharton's *House of Mirth* (1905). Indeed, the blunt, unironic moral seriousness of Howells, for example, would strike a discordant note today.

That countercultural literary, religious, and political imagination of the nineteenth century which pronounced Wall Street an excommunicant depended on the capacity to be profoundly shocked, on a sense of violation. But that capacity has shrunk in our own day, supplanted by an air of comic bemusement and ironic detachment.

At first glance that may seem wrong. The financial high jinks of the past quarter century have seemingly breathed new life into the image of Wall Street as the great immoralist. Scan the titles of some of some of the best-selling books about the Street during the recent past: *Liar's Poker, Predators' Ball, Den of Thieves, Dot.Con, Barbarians at the Gate, Bonfire of the Vanities, Bombardiers.* And this is not to mention movie "heroes" like Gordon Gekko or psychotic and criminal variations on Gekko's triumphalist and chilling amorality in movies and plays like *American Psycho, Boiler Room,* and *Other People's Money.* This suggests that the iconography of evil discoloring our ancestors' perception of Wall Street lives on . . . but it does so more as an afterlife.

An atmosphere of comic irony or knowing fatalism, or sometimes both, suffuses most of these books and movies. The "liars" morph into a bunch of wild and crazy Salomon fraternity brothers. The confidence men in *Bombardiers* are hilariously funny. But their schemes to securitize whole countries, to auction them off as IPOs, don't emit the infernal aroma the reader smells in Melville's equally amusing portrait of the Wall Street "bear" on the riverboat *Fidele*. Michael Milken's Predators living it up at the Beverly Hilton indulge voracious appetites as gargantuan as those of the old Robber Barons. But except in extremis, their chronicler grants them a pass for carrying out a necessary angioplasty on the clogged arteries of economic circulation. Those "Barbarians" storming the gates of RJR Nabisco are not a threat to Western civilization as once the Adamses and Godkin perceived Vanderbilt and Gould and Russell Sage to be. Rather they menace only Wall Street's old guard, engaging in a battle between titans whose moral significance is something less than titanic. And the "Vanities" Tom Wolfe skewers belong to "masters of the universe" so fragile and unprepossessing as to call into question their mastery of anything. It is difficult to see them as a serious moral threat to anyone but themselves, even harder to imagine them with Morgan's scary preternatural eyes looming up from some nonhuman abyss.

To perceive eyes in that way, the observer needs to feel him- or herself in the presence of the uncanny, to live with the fear of God and the Devil, even if those deities have been stripped of their supernatural attributes. When earlier generations of scandalized writers, hellfire preachers, and outraged tribunes of popular wrath peered into Wall Street and saw a whole bestiary of moral depravity, their eyesight underwent a kind of cultural magnification. These hedonists, idlers, parasites, and thieves appeared not only fascinating in their own right but players in a more global moral melodrama.

Beginning long ago and continuing through the New Deal, various forms of political opposition—Jeffersonian and then Jacksonian democracy, populism, Progressive-era reform, socialism, the antitrust movement, labor uprisings, the New Deal itself—lent a gravitas to this cultural persuasion and its moral confrontation with the Street. The withering away of these political insurgencies in the more recent past helps account for the weightlessness of the liars and thieves and masters of the universe of our own era. They survive as remnants, if that.

After FDR the moral animus directed at Wall Street subsided. For several decades the Street receded and then virtually vanished as a target of ethical anxiety. In one sense the disappearance of the Street for a long generation marked the collective triumph of those earlier cultural indictments and political insurgencies. Arguably they died nobly and of natural causes, having managed to curtail and inhibit Wall Street's worst breaches of public and private morality (not to mention the Street's political and economic wrongdoings). But the wheel continued to turn. When Kevin Phillips published *The Politics of Rich and Poor* in 1990 it caused a stir. Here a Republican apostate, famous for his strategic discovery of Nixon's "silent majority," denounced the Reagan revolution as the "triumph of upper class America." His catalogue of its sins would have been familiar to any late-nineteenth-century populist. Indeed, Phillips thought he sensed a rising movement against "the oligarchy" that would echo the thunderous anathemas of Bryan and other jeremiahs who proceeded and followed him. Phillips was convinced the 1990s would go down as a "watershed decade."[27]

It was not to be. The "new era" of the dot.com worshiped at the shrine of "shareholder value." Wall Street, once everybody's favorite immoralist, emerged instead as the paragon of economic virtue—a miraculous transformation if ever there was one. Even after the free-fall of the stock market and the cascade of financial scandals beginning with Enron, the temperature of public indignation remained low, hardly registering in the congressional elections of 2002. On the one hand, it is probably true that the Bush administration's failed attempt to privatize Social Security did indeed suffer as a result. A residual distrust of the Street and its moral imperfections remains and probably always will. Nonetheless, Wall Street the immoralist does not haunt the public imagination as for generations it once did.

Some way of dealing with Wall Street in our midst, an encompassing moral temperament once deeply ingrained in American culture has grown frail and sickly. Why? Not because an international conspiracy ate away at the country's moral innards. Henry Ford had it wrong, malignantly wrong. But the ethos of play and consumerism he found so repugnant in the 1920s no doubt has exercised in the decades since a sedative effect on the spiritual vigilance that once stigmatized the Street. For the moment at least, Wall Street has escaped the gulag.

Epilogue

Wall Street has been around for two centuries. (The street itself goes back to the founding days of Dutch colonial New York in the early 1600s, when it included a wooden wall to ward off the British, but the financial center began in the era of the American Revolution.) For most of those two hundred years there has been a great distance separating the Street from the American people. That gulf was political, social, and cultural all at once. The apparitions that attached themselves to Wall Street vividly captured this sense that the Street was the habitat of the abnormal. Certainly the aristocrat, the confidence man, and the immoralist were considered foreign matter, not native to the healthy American organism and dangerous to its survival. Even the hero, however much he was admired and endowed with a familial likeness to the pathfinder, frontiersman, and cowboy, was still a rare fig-ure, towering over the mass of men like a Napoleon.

During the past half century, and especially during the age of Ronald Reagan, that sense of estrangement has diminished. We can today talk about the democratization of Wall Street both as a reality and as a set of shared expectations in ways our ancestors would have found dubious. Can we add the image of Everyman to the gallery of Wall Street icons without seeming ludicrous?

For some people, ordinary citizens, the answer to that ques-tion has always been an unproblematic yes. According to this view, risk taking is an indigenous national character trait. And Americans have been especially blessed, a people of plenty whose daring exploits on behalf of material wealth have been richly re-warded. Wall Street, however much its reputation has rested on images of masses of wealth and alpine barriers of social exclusiv-ity, has at the same time presented itself as a casino, open to any-one bold or reckless enough to want to play. Money, after all, can function as a leveler as much as an upholder of hierarchies of power. Ancestry, breeding, education, religion, honorific titles all count for little or nothing when it comes to paying Wall Street's price of admission. That has been its plebian appeal to dreamers and schemers as far back as the early decades of the nineteenth century.

Except for a relative handful of people—a few of whom, like Jim Fisk or Daniel Drew, gained fame—this peculiar Wall Street version of the American dream remained a dream. Briefly, during the 1920s, it seemed about to become more tangible. Wall Street came to be associated in the popular mind with the flapper, bootleg gin, and jazz because its promise of fast money was an integral part of the era's new culture of play that captivated many middle-class Americans. On a less fanciful level, the number of people participating in the market grew considerably; they were not the mesmerized multitudes of historical legend but they still counted several million more than had previously ventured anywhere near the Street. But soon the great crash turned the dream into a nightmare.

Psychic recovery took longer than economic rebirth. A national preoccupation with security and an aversion to risk lasted for a long generation. But in one of the more fascinating ironies of recent American history, it was precisely this quest for security which helped make many ordinary people feel more at home on the Street. Unions, which until recently represented a considerable share of the workforce, were in the post–World War II era effective means for achieving economic security. Union pension funds, won through collective bargaining or accumulated as separate fraternal benefit accounts, soon ended up in the stock market as institutional investors joined the Street's principal players during the last quarter of the twentieth century. Meanwhile, the varieties of investment retirement vehicles proliferated for the middle class, not only for working-class trade unionists. By the end of the century roughly half of all American families had some stake in the market, mainly through their holdings in mutual funds and other forms of relatively risk-averse financial instruments.

By the 1990s many people, whose Depression-era mothers and fathers might cringe at the very thought of wagering anything on the stock market, had come to see it as an entirely reasonable place not only to make provision for their retirement but to finance college educations, a wedding, vacation homes, and ordinary big-ticket consumer items. Most of these people were passive participants. They entrusted their surplus capital to an array of investment advisers and institutions. Their ambitions were relatively modest, their instincts still conservative. They hardly resembled the daredevil speculators of Wall Street lore. Nonetheless, their very presence in such vast numbers made Wall Street seem middle-American in a way previously unimaginable.

And then there was the dot.com bubble. This did indeed invite the participation of those whose instincts were anything but prudent. Day traders, for example, imagined themselves as financial mavericks, riding the free range of the World Wide Web in hot pursuit of exotic treasures invisible to nearsighted, overly timid institutional investors, brokers, and investment house analysts. For the shirt-sleeved day trader, hooked up to a personal computer, often moonlighting from a day job as a truck driver or housewife, the appeal was psychic and immaterial as much as it was about the money: the thrill of the hunt, the gambler's high, thumbing one's nose at all those presumptuous "experts."

All of this and much more seemed peculiarly possible and rational thanks to the information superhighway. The outsized confidence of day traders (but not only day traders) was kept aloft by a new technology that promised to make information transparent and available to all, even the most esoteric information, even that encoded, arcane knowledge which for generations had been sequestered deep within the labyrinthine byways of the Street. No more insider trading because now everybody could be an insider, or so it seemed. Moreover, visions of the new technology, at least as advertised by its entrepreneurs and promoters in the media, were grandiose, approaching the metaphysical. Whether stock market exuberance was considered irrational by some and rational by others (or, as in the case of Alan Greenspan, both in succession), the conventional wisdom had it that an information-based economy would inaugurate a new era, one resting on a plateau of permanent prosperity, free of cyclic spasms—those booms followed by busts, with all their heart-breaking collateral damage. Hence all those absurd prices paid for newly minted stock at IPOs for Internet companies, especially, many of them more virtual than real, companies without profits, revenue, or even products.

It is hard to exaggerate how far the Street's aura reached during the glory years of the dot.com boom. Newspaper and magazine articles reported on ordinary people who dreamed of the market at night: an investor who said, "It's given me a feeling of control over my life I've never had before"; a woman who remarked that her newest romantic interest had "tremendous upside potential"; a dentist who confessed that he tracked his stocks between patient visits, sometimes even between X-rays and fillings. First came class consciousness, then the royal road to the unconscious; now there was "Dow consciousness." Once there was a Depression generation, then a Sixties generation; now there was a Dow generation. For some years it became virtually impossible to turn on the TV or radio, plug into the Internet, or even attend a baseball game without joining an all-day, every-day open house hosted at Broad and Wall Streets.[1]

But the dot.cometh and it also goeth away, as it did at warp speed with the crash of 2000. It turned out that the expectations and exuberance were indeed irrational. Market panics were by no means a thing of the past. And the Enron scandal and the cascade of disasters that followed for years afterward, affecting many of the leading financial and corporate institutions of the country, made it woefully clear that insider trading was also alive and all too well. It is hard to predict whether this will have a lasting impact on Wall Street's most recent iconic incarnation as Everyman. Certainly, everybody is now forewarned that the Street's less savory presences remain at large. Whether Americans will continue nonetheless to find in Wall Street a welcoming place to indulge their romance with risk and dreams of universal abundance remains to be seen.

Notes

ONE

The Aristocrat

1. Eric Homberger, *Mrs. Astor's New York: Money and Social Power in a Gilded Age* (New York, 2002), 49–50.

2. Cathy Mason, "Public Vices, Private Benefits: William Duer and His Circle, 1776–1792," in William Pencok and Conrad Edick Wright, eds., *New York and the Rise of American Capitalism: Economic Development and the Social and Political History of an American State, 1780–1870* (New York, 1989); see also Stanley Elkins and Eric McKittrick, *The Age of Federalism: The Early American Republic, 1788–1800* (New York, 1993).

3. Mason, "Public Vices."

4. Alexander Hamilton, "The First Report on the Public Credit," January 14, 1790, and "The Second Report on the Public Credit," January 16, 1795, in Samuel McKee, Jr., *Alexander Hamilton Papers: Paper on Public Credit, Commerce, and Finance* (New York, 1934); Herbert E. Sloan, *Principle and Interest: Thomas Jefferson and the Problem of Debt* (New York, 1995), 110.

5. Mason, "Public Vices"; Homberger, *Mrs. Astor's New York*, 46–50.

6. Alexander Hamilton, "Observations on Certain Documents Contained in nos. 5 & 6 of 'The History of the United States for the Year 1796' in

Which Charges of Speculation Against Alexander Hamilton, Late Secretary of the Treasury, Is Fully Refuted by Himself" (Philadelphia, 1797).

7. Thomas Jefferson to the President of the United States (George Washington), May 23, 1792, in Merrill Peterson, ed., *Thomas Jefferson: Writings* (New York, 1984), 986.

8. Washington, quoted in Mason, "Public Vices."

9. Philip Freneau, quoted in Karen Weyler, "A Speculating Spirit: Trade, Speculation, and Gambling in Early American Fiction," *American Literature* 31, no. 3 (1996); Thomas Jefferson, "The Anas, 1791–1806," in Peterson, *Jefferson: Writings;* Madison, quoted in Elkins and McKittrick, *Age of Federalism*, 243; Adams, quoted in Vernon Louis Parrington, *Main Currents in American Thought: An Interpretation of Literature from the Beginnings to 1920*, 3 vols. (New York, 1927–30), 1:314.

10. A Philadelphia citizen, quoted in Elkins and McKittrick, *Age of Federalism*, 460; Madison, quoted in Elkins and McKittrick, *Age of Federalism*, 243.

11. Hamilton, quoted in Gary J. Kornblith and John Murrin, "The Dilemmas of Ruling Elites in Revolutionary America," in Steve Fraser and Gary Gerstle, eds., *Ruling America: A History of Wealth and Power in a Democracy* (Cambridge, Mass., 2005); Hamilton, quoted in Sloan, *Principle and Interest*, 138; Dixon Wecter, *The Saga of American Society: A Record of Social Aspirations, 1607–1937* (New York, 1937), 8.

12. Homberger, *Mrs. Astor's New York*, 46–50; Marvin Gelfand, "The Street," *American Heritage* 38, no. 7 (1987); Wecter, *Saga of American Society*, 8; Jay, quoted in Carl Becker, *The United States: An Experiment in Democracy* (New Brunswick, N.J.), 86.

13. Tom Watson, "Wall Street Conspiracies Against the American Nation," *New York World Sunday Magazine*, October 10, 1896.

14. James K. Medberry, *Men and Mysteries of Wall Street* (1870; rpt., New York, 1968), 10–11, 194–95, 196–97, 247; observer, quoted in Maury Klein, *The Life and Legend of Jay Gould* (Baltimore, 1986), 70.

15. "Wall Street in War Time, " *Harper's New Monthly*, December 1864– May 1865.

16. "One of the Upper Ten Thousand," illustration in Carl Bode, ed., *Documents in American Civilization: American Life in the 1840s* (New York, 1967); William Worthington Fowler, *Ten Years in Wall Street; or, Revelations of Inside Life and Experience on 'Change* (1870; rpt., New York, 1971), 42. See also Edith Wharton, *A Backward Glance* (New York, 1934).

17. Lloyd, quoted in Chester McArthur Destler, *American Radicalism, 1865–1901: Essays and Documents* (Menasha, Wis., 1946), 219.
18. Charles Francis Adams and Henry Adams, *Chapters of Erie* (1886; rpt., Ithaca, N.Y., 1956), 3, 8, 10, 33, 95, 98.
19. William Graham Sumner, *What Social Classes Owe Each Other* (1883; rpt., London, 1961).
20. Sven Beckert, "The Making of New York City's Bourgeoisie, 1850–1886" (Ph.D. diss., Columbia University, 1995), 354; Thomas Kessner, *Capital City: New York City and the Men Behind America's Rise to Economic Dominance, 1860–1900* (New York, 2003), 247–48; Mary Elizabeth Lease, quoted in Edward Herbert Mazur, *Minyans for a Prairie City: The Politics of Chicago Jewry, 1850–1940* (New York, 1990).
21. Ignatius Donnelley, *Caesar's Column: A Story of the Twentieth Century* (Cambridge, Mass., 1960), 246.
22. Carl Smith, *Urban Disorder and the Shape of Belief: The Great Chicago Fire, the Haymarket Bomb, and the Model Town of Pullman* (Chicago, 1995), 61.
23. George E. Mowry, *The Era of Theodore Roosevelt and the Birth of Modern America, 1900–1912* (New York, 1962); Teddy Roosevelt to Henry Cabot Lodge, November 14, 1906, in *Letters of Theodore Roosevelt: Selections from the Correspondence of Theodore Roosevelt and Henry Cabot Lodge, 1884–1918* (New York, 1925); William H. Horbaugh, ed., *The Writings of Theodore Roosevelt* (New York, 1967), 86, 423–32.
24. Robert H. Wiebe, "The House of Morgan and the Executive, 1905–13," *American Historical Review* 65 (October 1959); Jean Strouse, *Morgan: American Financier* (New York, 1999), 440–41; Morgan, quoted in Stephen Birmingham, *Our Crowd: The Great Jewish Families of New York* (New York, 1967), 203.
25. Roosevelt, quoted in Mowry, *Era of Theodore Roosevelt*, 98; Roosevelt, quoted in Wecter, *Saga of American Society*, 109.
26. Morgan, quoted by Frederick Lewis Allen, *Lords of Creation* (New York, 1935), 160.
27. Louis D. Brandeis, *Other People's Money and How the Bankers Use It*, ed. Melvin I. Urofsky (New York, 1995), 27, 33, 68–69, 70–71.
28. Woodrow Wilson, *The New Freedom* (New York, 1913), 177; Wilson, quoted by Richard Hofstadter, *The Paranoid Style in American Politics and Other Essays* (Cambridge, Mass., 1952), 208; Wilson, acceptance speech, Democratic Party convention, August 7, 1912, in Arthur M. Schlesinger,

Jr., and Roger Bruns, eds., *Congress Investigates: A Documented History,* *1792–1974* (New York, 1975), vol. 3.

29. George Reynolds, quoted in *Current Opinion,* February 1913.
30. Schlesinger and Bruns, *Congress Investigates,* 2264–65, 2267–68, 2295–98, 2343.
31. Wecter, *Saga of American Society,* 124; *New York Times,* April 10, 11, 12, 1913; the Reverend William Wilkinson, quoted in Sigmund Diamond, *The Reputation of the American Businessman* (Cambridge, Mass., 1955), chap. 4.
32. Franklin Delano Roosevelt, Inaugural Address, in Roosevelt, *Looking Forward* (New York, 1933), 263, 265; Russell De Buhite and David Levy, eds., *FDR's Fireside Chats* (Norman, Okla., 1992), fireside chats of March 12, 1933, October 22, 1933, September 30, 1934.
33. Letter from FDR quoted in Jordan A. Schwarz, *Liberal: Adolph Berle and the Vision of an American Era* (New York, 1987), 108.
34. Schlesinger and Bruns, *Congress Investigates,* "The Pecora Wall Street Exposé,"2563, 2566, 2570, 2572; "Big Bankers Gambling Mania," *Literary Digest,* March 11, 1935; N. R. Danielion, "The Stock Market and the Public," *Atlantic Monthly,* October 1933; Father Coughlin and Huey Long, quoted in Alan Brinkley, "Dissidents and Demagogues," in Colin Gordon, ed., *Major Problems in American History, 1920–45* (Boston, 1999), 385, 387.
35. Edmund Wilson, "Sunshine Charlie," in Wilson, *The American Earthquake: A Documentary of the Twenties and Thirties* (New York, 1958).
36. Jack Morgan, quoted in Wecter, *Saga of American Society,* 141.
37. John Brooks, *Once in Golconda: A True Drama of Wall Street, 1920–38* (New York, 1969), 180–82.
38. *New York Times Magazine,* quoted in Haynes Johnson, *Sleepwalking Through History: America in the Reagan Years* (New York, 1992), 196.

T W O
The Confidence Man

1. Mark Twain, quoted in Walter Fuller Taylor, *The Economic Novel in America* (New York, 1964), 126.
2. A. J. Liebling, "High Finance in the Gilded Age: The Great Diamond Hoax," in Richard A. Bartlett, ed., *The Gilded Age: America, 1865–1900: Interpretive Articles and Documentary Sources* (Boston, 1969), originally published in the *New Yorker,* November 16, 1940, as "The American Golconda."

3. Washington Irving, quoted in Bray Hammond, *Banks and Politics in America: From the Revolution to the Civil War* (Princeton, 1957), 438; Vernon Louis Parrington, *Main Currents in American Literature: From the Beginnings to 1920* (New York, 1927–30), 2: 204, 208–10; Ralph Waldo Emerson, "The Conduct of Life," quoted in Patricia O'Toole, *Money and Morals* (New York, 1998), 93.
4. Jeremiah Church, quoted in Marvin Myers, *The Jacksonian Persuasion: Politics and Belief* (Stanford, 1957), 138.
5. Charles Dickens, *American Notes and Pictures from Italy* (London, 1987); Charles Dickens, *Martin Chuzzlewit* (New York, 1965), 376–77, 383.
6. George Foster, *New York by Gaslight and Other Urban Sketches* (1850; rpt., Berkeley, Calif., 1990), 131, 220–21, 226–27.
7. Johannes Bergmann, "The Original Confidence Man," *American Quarterly* 31, no. 3 (fall 1960).
8. Herman Melville, *The Confidence Man: His Masquerade* (New York, 1967), 67–71.
9. See Ann Fabian, *Card Sharps, Dream Books, and Bucket Shops: Gambling in Nineteenth-Century America* (Ithaca, N.Y., 1990), 188, 191, 195; Cedric B. Cowing, *Populists, Plungers, and Progressives: A Social History of Commodity Speculation, 1890–1930* (Princeton, 1965), 28–30; Edwin Lefevre, "Gambling in Bucket Shops," *Harper's Weekly*, May 11, 1901.
10. Edward G. Burrows and Mike Wallace, *Gotham: A History of New York City to 1898* (New York, 1999), 1042–43.
11. See Ellis Paxson Oberholtzer, *Jay Cooke: Financier of the Civil War* (Philadelphia, 1907), 2:224–25, 233–34, 238, 240, 243, 295, 301, 309; John Steele Gordon, *The Great Game: The Emergence of Wall Street as a World Power, 1653–2000* (New York, 1999), 143; Edward Chancellor, *Devil Take the Hindmost: A History of Financial Speculation* (New York, 1999), 184.
12. The best account of the Erie wars is John Steele Gordon, *The Scarlet Woman of Wall Street: Jay Gould, Jim Fisk, Cornelius Vanderbilt, the Erie Railway Wars, and the Birth of Wall Street* (New York, 1988); see also W. A. Swanberg, *Jim Fisk: The Career of an Improbable Rascal* (New York, 1959). The best account of the Gold Ring is Kenneth D. Ackerman, *The Gold Ring: Jim Fisk, Jay Gould, and Black Friday, 1869* (New York, 1988).
13. Mark Twain and Charles Dudley Warner, *The Gilded Age: A Tale of Today* (1873; New York, 1994); see also Chancellor, *Devil Take the Hindmost*, 170; Taylor, *Economic Novel*, 130–31.

14. Robert Sobel, *The Great Bull Market: Wall Street in the 1920s* (New York, 1968), 17–20.

15. This and the following profiles from John Brooks, *Once in Golconda: A True Drama of Wall Street, 1920–38* (New York, 1969), 78, 122; Mark Smith, *Towards Rational Exuberance: The Evolution of the Modern Stock Market* (New York, 2001), 79, 136; Gordon Thomas and Max Morgan-Witt, *The Day the Bubble Burst: A Social History of the Wall Street Crash of 1929* (New York, 1979), 20; Tom Schactman, *The Day America Crashed* (New York, 1979), 52; Sobel, *Great Bull Market*, 85–87.

16. John Kenneth Galbraith, *The Great Crash 1929* (Boston, 1997), 20–21, 53–54, 60–66; Frederick Lewis Allen, *Only Yesterday: An Informal History of the 1920s* (New York, 1931), 271–72, 322; observer of stock market as sport, quoted in Brooks, *Once in Golconda*, 72.

17. Chancellor, *Devil Take the Hindmost*, 202; Schactman, *Day America Crashed*, 43; Thomas and Morgan-Witt, *Day the Bubble Burst*, 282; Arthur M. Schlesinger, Jr., and Roger Bruns, eds., *Congress Investigates: A Documented History, 1792–1974* (New York, 1975), 3:2576, 2721; Cowling, *Populists, Plungers, and Progressives*, 233, 242.

18. Brooks, *Once in Golconda*, 61, 129, 273, 287; Galbraith, *Great Crash*, 102, 161–65; Thomas K. McCraw, *Prophets of Regulation: Charles Francis Adams, Louis D. Brandeis, James M. Landis, Alfred E. Kahn* (Cambridge, Mass., 1984), 196.

19. Schactman, *Day America Crashed*, 18; Thomas Lamont, quoted in Thomas and Morgan-Witts, *Day the Bubble Burst*, 345, and see also 70, 78, 134.

20. Kathleen Odean, *High Steppers, Fallen Angels, and Lollipops: Wall Street Slang* (New York, 1988), 131.

21. Scientist interviewed by *Forbes* quoted in Robert Teitelman, *Gene Dreams: Wall Street, Academia, and the Rise of Biotechnology* (New York, 1989), 27; *Wall Street Journal*, quoted in David Colbert, *Eyewitness to Wall Street: Four Hundred Years of Dreams, Schemes, Busts, and Booms* (New York, 2001), 327; Abby Joseph Cohen, quoted in Robert Shiller, *Irrational Exuberance* (New York, 2000), 74, and see also 28, 30; Smith, *Toward Rational Exuberance*, 255; John Cassidy, "Pricking the Bubble," *New Yorker*, August 17, 1998; John Cassidy, "The Fountainhead," in David Remnick, ed., *The New Gilded Age: The New Yorker Looks at the Culture of Affluence* (New York, 2000).

22. *New York Times*, November 2, 1999, and August 23, 1999; Colbert, *Eyewitness*, 330.

23. Po Bronson, *Bombardiers* (New York, 1995), 153, 223. See also Colbert, *Eyewitness*, 235; Haynes Johnson, *Sleepwalking Through History: America in the Reagan Years* (New York, 1991), 431–33; Michael Lewis, *Liar's Poker: Rising Through the Wreckage on Wall Street* (New York, 1989).
24. William D. Nordhaus, "The Story of the Bubble," *New York Review of Books*, January 15, 2004.
25. Louis Lapham, quoted in Kevin Phillips, *Wealth and Democracy: A Political History of the American Rich* (New York, 2002), 405.

THREE

The Hero

1. British observer, quoted in Dixon Wecter, *The Saga of American Society: A Record of Social Aspiration, 1607–1937* (New York, 1937), 142; *New York Herald*, quoted in H. W. Brands, *Masters of Enterprise* (New York, 1999), 25.
2. "The Vanderbilts," in Henry Nash Smith, ed., *Documents in American Civilization: Popular Culture and Industrialization, 1865–1900* (New York, 1967), 88. The material about Vanderbilt in the following paragraphs is from this source.
3. Ron Chernow, *The House of Morgan: An American Banking Dynasty and the Rise of Modern Finance* (New York, 1990), 7; James K. Medberry, *Men and Mysteries of Wall Street* (1870; rpt., New York, 1968), 157; John Steele Gordon, *The Scarlet Woman of Wall Street: Jay Gould, Jim Fisk, Cornelius Vanderbilt, the Erie Railway Wars, and the Birth of Wall Street* (New York, 1988), 91, 206, 309, 318, 332, 337, 374–75; *Harper's Weekly*, September 25, 1869; Sigmund Diamond, *The Reputation of the American Businessman* (Cambridge, Mass., 1955), 55, 61–62, 69, 72.
4. On Fisk, see William Worthington Fowler, *Ten Years in Wall Street; or, Revelations of Inside Life and Experience on 'Change* (1870; rpt., New York, 1971), 482; Jean Curtis Webber, "The Capital of Capitalism," *American Heritage* 24, no. 1 (1972); Stuart H. Holbrook, *The Age of Moguls* (New York, 1953), 22–23, 34, 41, 43, 46; W. A. Swanberg, *Jim Fisk: The Career of an Improbable Rascal* (New York, 1959), 7–8, 26, 169, 171.
5. David Nasaw, *Andrew Carnegie* (New York, 2006).
6. James D. McCabe, *Great Fortunes and How They Were Made* (New York, 1870), and quoted in Wecter, *Saga of American Society*, 197–98; Diamond, *Reputation of the American Businessman*, 55, 61–62, 69, 72. These characterizations can be found in numerous books, including Kenneth D. Ack-

erman, *The Gold Ring: Jim Fisk, Jay Gould, and Black Friday, 1869* (New York, 1988), Holbrook, *Age of Moguls*, and Thomas Kessner, *Capital City: New York City and the Men Behind America's Rise to Economic Dominance, 1860–1900* (New York, 2001).

7. Theodore P. Greene, *American Heroes: The Changing Models of Success in American Magazines* (New York, 1970), 110, 112; David Black, *The King of Fifth Avenue: The Fortunes of August Belmont* (New York, 1981).

8. William Graham Sumner, quoted in Richard Hofstadter, *Social Darwinism in American Thought* (Boston, 1992), 58.

9. Theodore Dreiser, *The Financier* (New York, 1967), 8–9; Dreiser, *The Titan* (New York, 1965), 397–98; Dreiser, *The Stoic* (New York, 1947).

10. Obituaries from *New York World, New York Tribune, Harper's Weekly,* all quoted in Diamond, *Reputation of American Businessman,* chap. 4; *New York Times,* April 10, 11, 12, 1913.

11. Nasaw, *Carnegie,* 474.

12. Chernow, *House of Morgan,* 38, 67–69; Jean Strouse, *Morgan: American Financier* (New York, 1999), 6, 261, 320.

13. James Livingston, *Origins of the Federal Reserve System: Money, Class, and Corporate Capitalism, 1890–1913* (Ithaca, N.Y., 1986), 51, 56, 58; Thomas H. Nevins and Marion V. Sears, "The Rise of the Market for Industrial Securities, 1887–1902," *Business History Review* 29 (1955); "Final Report of the United States Industrial Commission" (Washington, D.C., 1902), 19:616–19; Thomas Cochran and Warren Miller, *The Age of Enterprise: A Social History of Industrial America* (New York, 1942), 192–93; Vincent P. Carosso, *Investment Banking in America: A History* (Cambridge, Mass., 1970), 47–50, 140–44; Strouse, *Morgan,* 320, 395.

14. John Steele Gordon, "The Magnitude of J. P. Morgan," *American Heritage,* July–August 1989; Jean Strouse, "The Brilliant Bail-Out," *New Yorker,* November 23, 1998; Bernard Berenson, quoted in Strouse, *Morgan,* 589, and see also 582.

15. Carosso, *Investment Banking,* 222–23; John Steele Gordon, *The Great Game: The Emergence of Wall Street as a World Power, 1653–2000* (New York, 1999), 202, 208; Cochran and Miller, *Age of Enterprise,* 298–300; Alexander Dana Noyes, *The War Period of American Finance, 1908–1925* (New York, 1926), 7, 88, 106.

16. Stephen L. Harris, *Duty, Honor, Privilege: New York's Silk Stocking Regiment and the Breaking of the Hindenburg Line* (Washington, D.C., 2001), 295, 338.

17. See *Manhattan Inc.,* September 1984, July 1985, September 1987, among

many other issues; Edward Chancellor, *Devil Take the Hindmost: A History of Financial Speculation* (New York, 1999), 254, 264; Connie Bruck, *The Predators' Ball: The Inside Story of Drexel Burnham and the Rise of the Junk Bond Raiders* (New York, 1989), 245, 270; Haynes Johnson, *Sleepwalking Through History: America in the Reagan Years* (New York, 1991), 195, 215, 225–26; Ken Auletta, *Greed and Glory on Wall Street: The Fall of the House of Lehman* (New York, 1986); *Manhattan Inc.*, June 1987; Michael Lewis, *Liar's Poker: Rising Through the Wreckage on Wall Street* (New York, 1989).

18. Revisionist biographies of the era include Maury Klein, *The Life and Legend of Jay Gould* (Baltimore, 1986), Lloyd J. Mercer, *E. H. Harriman: Master Railroader* (Boston, 1985), and Ron Chernow, *The House of Morgan: An American Banking Dynasty and the Rise of Big Business* (New York, 1990). The trend would continue through the 1990s with new biographies of Morgan by Jean Strouse, of John D. Rockefeller by Ron Chernow, and of Harriman by Maury Klein and histories of Wall Street and big business by John Steele Gordon, Thomas Kessner, and Charles Geisst, among others.

19. Milken admirer, quoted in Bruck, *Predators' Ball*, 84, and see also 19, 84–85, 93, 95, 270; Auletta, *Greed and Glory*; Kevin Phillips, *Wealth and Democracy: A Political History of the American Rich* (New York, 2002), 366.

20. Kevin Phillips variously calls this the "financialization of the economy" and the "collectivization of risk" (not entirely the same thing) in *Wealth and Democracy*, 93, 95–98; Joseph Schumpeter, *The Theory of Economic Development* (New York, 1961), 126; Robert Brenner, *The Boom and the Bubble: The United States in the World Economy* (New York, 2000), 81, 86, 88; Kevin Phillips, *The Politics of Rich and Poor: Wealth and the American Electorate in the Reagan Aftermath* (New York, 1990), 70, 171–72, 174.

FOUR

The Immoralist

1. *New York Times*, quoted in Irving Katz, *August Belmont: A Political Biography* (New York, 1968), 143–45; David Black, *The King of Fifth Avenue: The Fortunes of August Belmont* (New York, 1981), 257.

2. Henry Ford, *The International Jew* (Dearborn, Mich., 1922), originally a series of articles published in the *Dearborn Independent* between 1920 and 1922 under the title "The Jewish Question"; Albert Lee, *Henry Ford and the Jews* (New York, 1980); Leo P. Ribuffo, "Henry Ford and the 'Inter-

national Jew,'" *American Jewish History* 60 (June 1980); David L. Lewis, "Henry Ford's Anti-Semitism and Its Repercussions," *Michigan Journal of History* 24 (January 1984).

3. Thomas Jefferson, quoted in John Steele Gordon, *The Great Game: The Emergence of Wall Street as a World Power, 1653–2000* (New York, 1999), 21.

4. Cotton Mather, quoted in Wayne Westbrook, *Wall Street in the American Novel* (New York, 1980), 8.

5. Poem excerpt quoted in Karen Weyler, "A Speculating Spirit: Trade, Speculation, and Gambling in Early American Fiction," *Early American Literature* 31, no. 3 (1996), and see this article for references to *Dorval; or, The Speculator;* Thomas Jefferson, "The Anas, 1791–1806," in Merrill Peterson, ed., *Thomas Jefferson: Writings* (New York, 1984).

6. Ann Fabian, *Card Sharps, Dream Books, and Bucket Shops: Gambling in Nineteenth-Century America* (Ithaca, N.Y., 1990), 6–7, 44, 61; Patricia Cline Cohen, "Unregulated Youth: Masculinity and Murder in the 1830s City," *Radical History Review* (winter 1992).

7. *Frank Leslie's Illustrated Newspaper,* September 12, 14, 19, and October 3, 10, 17, 24, 1857; *New York Ledger,* July 27, 1850, May 22 and October 17, 24, 1857; Charles Frederick Briggs, *The Adventures of Harry Franco: A Tale of the Great Panic* (1839; rpt., New York, 1969).

8. George Foster, *New York by Gaslight and Other Urban Sketches* (1850; rpt., Berkeley, Calif., 1990), 131, 220–21, 226–27.

9. Foster, *New York by Gaslight;* George Lippard, *The Quaker City; or, The Monks of Monk Hall* (Amherst, Mass., 1970).

10. President Jackson, quoted in Bray Hammond, *Banks and Politics in America: From the Revolution to the Civil War* (Princeton, 1957), 430–31; President Jackson's Farewell Address, March 4, 1837, in Francis Newton Thorpe, *The Statesmanship of Andrew Jackson* (New York, 1904).

11. All quotations cited in Maury Klein, *The Life and Legend of Jay Gould* (Baltimore, 1986).

12. *New York World,* quoted in Klein, *Life and Legend,* 484.

13. Joseph Pulitzer, in *New York World,* and *New York Times,* quoted in Klein, *Life and Legend,* 484, 3, and see also 217, 477; James R. Keene, quoted by Edward Chancellor, *Devil Take the Hindmost: A History of Financial Speculation* (New York, 1999), 178.

14. Henry Adams, *Democracy: An American Novel* (New York, 2003), 1, 6, 8–9.

15. Charles Francis Adams and Henry Adams, *Chapters of Erie* (1886; rpt., Ithaca, N.Y., 1956), 3, 8, 10, 33, 95, 98.

16. Henry Adams, quoted in Michael N. Dobkowski, *The Tarnished Dream: The Basis of American Anti-Semitism* (Westport, Conn., 1979), 122, 125.
17. Brooks Adams, quoted in Dobkowski, *Tarnished Dream*, 126.
18. E. L. Godkin in *The Nation*, November 18, 1869, January 11, 1872, September 15, 25, 1873, October 2, 9, 1873, November 6, 1873.
19. Irwin G. Wylie, *The Self-Made Man in America: The Myth of Rags to Riches* (Glencoe, Ill., 1954), 56, 65.
20. Henry Ward Beecher, quoted in Wayne Westbrook, *Wall Street in the American Novel* (New York, 1980), 39; Beecher, quoted by W. A. Swanberg, *Jim Fisk: The Career of an Improbable Rascal* (New York, 1959), 113; Beecher, quoted in Wylie, *Self-Made Man*, 70; Henry Ward Beecher, "The Deceitfulness of Riches," quoted in David Mark Wheeler, "Perceptions of Money and Wealth on Gilded Age Stages: A Study of Four Long Run Productions" (Ph.D. diss., University of Oregon, 1986), 62.
21. Washington Gladdens, "The Three Dangers: Moral Aspects of Social Questions," in *Applied Christianity and Moral Aspects of Social Questions* (1886; rpt., New York, 1976), 203–5.
22. Morton Keller, *The Art and Politics of Thomas Nast* (New York, 1968); *Thomas Nast: Cartoons and Illustrations with Text by Thomas Nast St. Hill* (New York, 1974), plate 85; "This Street Is Closed for Repairs," cartoon cited in C. Vann Woodward, "The Lowest Ebb," *American Heritage* 8 (1957); New-York Historical Society exhibition, "Games," 2001.
23. Jan W. Dietrichson, *The Image of Money in the American Novel of the Gilded Age* (New York, 1969), 336; J. W. DeForest, *Honest John Vane* (1875; rpt., State College, Pa., 1960), 84, 124, 159; Howard, quoted in Wheeler, "Perceptions of Money and Wealth on Gilded Age Stages."
24. William Dean Howells, *A Hazard of New Fortunes* (New York, 1965), 225–27.
25. Robert H. Walker, "The Poet and the Robber Baron," *American Quarterly* 13, no. 4 (1961).
26. *Sioux Falls Daily Argus*, quoted in Sigmund Diamond, *The Reputation of the American Businessman* (Cambridge, Mass., 1955), 89.
27. Kevin Phillips, *The Politics of Rich and Poor: Wealth and the American Electorate in the Reagan Aftermath* (New York, 1990), xvii, xviii, xxiii.

Epilogue

1. Matthew Klam, "Riding the Mo in the Lime Green Glow," *New York Times Sunday Magazine*, November 21, 1999; Chris Smith, "How the

Stock Market Swallowed New York," *New York Magazine,* October 3, 1998; "Stunning Stock Action Pervades New York Culture," *USA Today,* March 30, 1999; "Some Abandon Water Cooler for Internet Stock Trading," *New York Times,* May 29, 1999; "People of the Bull," *Business Week,* April 12, 1999.

Acknowledgments

It has been a great pleasure to prepare this book for the Icons of America series of Yale University Press. For that opportunity I want to first thank my good friend Rochelle Gurstein. Rochelle knew my previous work on Wall Street and also knew about the series, and she suggested that we would make a good fit. Mark Crispin Miller was excited about adding a book on Wall Street to the series and got me excited about all the other fascinating subjects lined up to appear there. John Donatich and Jonathan Brent welcomed me to the Press with great enthusiasm. Jonathan has been a responsive and thoughtful editor throughout, and I have come to rely on his advice. I also want to thank his assistant Annelise Finnegan, who has been invariably helpful with many important details. Susan Laity did a superb job as my line editor, catching many an instance of overwriting and other literary sins.

She is a true master of her craft. Evan Daniel, a graduate student who knows his way around picture archives, tracked down the graphics that appear in the text. Finally, I want to thank my friend and longtime colleague Gary Gerstle for taking time to read the manuscript when it was nearly done and suggesting some good ways that it might be made better.

Index

Adams, Brooks, 158–59
Adams, Charles Francis, 33, 157, 158
Adams, Evangeline, 86
Adams, Henry, 33, 57, 157, 158
Adams, John, 19
Adelphia, 91–92
Alexander, William, 13
American Revolution, 13, 144
anti-Semitism, 155; of Henry
   Adams, 158–59; of Henry Ford,
   136–38, 140; and Wall Street,
   136, 140–42
antitrust legislation, 40, 42
aristocracy, 4–5, 51–53, 175; Americans' fears regarding, 17–19,
   21–22, 33–34, 52, 142–43,
   145–46; and capitalists, 23;
   ostentatious manifestations of,
   26–29; power embedded in,
   30–34

Arnold, Philip, 55–58
Art of War (Sun Tzu), 126
Arthur Andersen, 91–92
Astor, John Jacob, 61

banks, 31–32, 119, 149–50
Beecher, Henry Ward, 162
Bellamy, Edward, 37
Belmont, August, 27, 56, 57, 111–12,
   136
Belmont-Rothschild interests, 31,
   119, 136
Bennett, James Gordon, 67–68
Berenson, Bernard, 121–22
Berle, Adolph, 47
Biddle, Nicholas, 149
Boesky, Ivan, 51–52, 90, 104, 127
Boiler Room (film), 88–89
Bolsheviks, as threat to Wall Street,
   137, 138–39

Bombardiers (Bronson), 89–91, 170
bond traders, 126
Bonfire of the Vanities (Wolfe), 132
Brady, "Diamond Jim," 104
Brandeis, Louis, 42–43, 49
Bronson, Po, 89–91
Brown Brothers, 31
Bryan, William Jennings, 24, 117
bucket shops, 70–71
Bush, George W., 93–94
Butler, Benjamin, 56

Caesar's Column (Donnelley), 37–38
capitalism: and American aristocracy, 23; Bolsheviks as threat to,
138–39; as promoted by Wall
Street, 1, 141
Carnegie, Andrew, 36–37, 105,
109
Chrysler, Walter, 81
Church, Jeremiah, 62
Cleveland, Grover, 25, 33
Cohen, Abby Joseph, 88
Confidence Man (Melville), 68–70,
170
confidence men, 4–6, 170, 175; in
fiction, 63–64, 68–70, 76–78;
during the Jazz Age, 78–87; in
market society, 58–61; during
the 1990s, 87–91; and paper
economy, 60; and railroad speculation, 71–76
consumerism, 141
Conwell, Russell, 161
Cooke, Jay, 72–73, 105
Coughlin, Father Charles, 48
Crash of *1929*, 4, 46, 78, 177
Crédit Mobilier scandal, 77, 158

day traders, 178
Depression. *See* Great Depression
Dickens, Charles, 63–64
Dillon Read, 31
Donnelley, Ignatius, 37
dot.com bubble. *See* Internet stock
bubble
Dreiser, Theodore, 112–15
Drew, Daniel, 30, 74–76, 100, 111,
161
Drexel Burnham Lambert, 90,
127–28
Duer, Lady Kitty, 13, 15
Duer, William, 11–13, 15, 16,
19–21, 22, 53, 144
Dunlap, Al, 124
Durant, William Crapo, 81

Edelman, Asher, 126
Emerson, Ralph Waldo, 61–62, 69
Enron, 9, 91
Europe, relation with United
States, 122–23

Fish, Mrs. Hamilton, 27
Fisher, Irving, 85
Fisk, "Jubilee Jim," 6, 30, 74–76,
100, 101–3, 105, 111, 115, 158
Fitzgerald, F. Scott, 86
Ford, Henry, 109, 135–36, 173;
anti-Semitism of, 136–38, 140
Foster, George, 65, 148
Fowler, William, 29
Freneau, Philip, 18
Frick, Henry Clay, 130

gambling: as sin, 143–44, 168; Wall
Street associated with, 139–40,
146, 163, 176

Gilded Age, 23, 129–30, 150–51, 155–56, 169–70; second (in the 1980s), 52, 126–31
Gilded Age (Twain and Warner), 26, 55, 77–78
Gladdens, Washington, 163
Glass-Steagall Act, 49, 93
Godkin, E. L., 111, 157, 160
Gould, Jay, 6, 30, 36, 74, 75–76, 100, 105, 106, 126, 151–54, 162
Graff, Lya, 50–51
Grant, Ulysses "Buck," Jr., 71
Grant, Ulysses S, 5, 32, 71
Great Depression, 9, 46, 78
Great Diamond Hoax of *1872*, 55–58
Great Gatsby (Fitzgerald), 86
Greeley, Horace, 62
Greenspan, Alan, 88, 179

Hamilton, Alexander, 13–16, 19–21, 145
Harding, Warren G., 136
Harriman, Edward, 105, 126
Harriman Brothers, 31
Haymarket bombing of *1886*, 36
Hazard of New Fortunes (Howells), 165–66, 169
Hearst, William Randolph, 67
hero, 6–7, 104–15, 130–33, 175–76; in fiction, 112–15, 132; Fisk as, 101–3; in the late twentieth century, 129–32; media adulation of, 110–12, 125; Milken as, 124–25, 128–29; Morgan as, 115–22, 130–31; Napoleon as, 100–101; scholarly studies of, 126; and the Silk

Stocking Regiment, 123–24; Vanderbilt as, 97–100
Hill, James, 105
Homestead Strike of *1892*, 36–37
Hoover, Herbert, 85
House of Mirth (Wharton), 169
House of Morgan, 31, 50–51
Howells, William Dean, 165–66, 169

Icahn, Carl, 9, 51–52, 127
immoralists, 7–8, 133, 139–43, 175; and aristocracy, 145–46; as depicted by authors and journalists, 145–49, 151–52; and gambling, 143–44; as perceived by the middle classes, 154–57; political response to, 166–68
insider trading, 90, 179, 180
International Jew (Ford), 136–38
Internet stock bubble, 59, 87–89, 94, 178, 179–80
investment banks: power held by, 31–32. *See also* Wall Street
investment pools, 81–82
Irving, Washington, 61

Jackson, Andrew, 146, 149–50
Jay, John, 22
Jazz Age, 59
Jefferson, Thomas, 4, 15–16, 142, 145–46
Jerome, Leonard, 27
Jewett, Helen, 146
Jews. *See* anti-Semitism
Josephson, Matthew, 152
junk bonds, 124, 128, 129. *See also* Milken, Michael

Keene, James R., 44, 153
Kennedy, Joseph, 79, 80, 104
Kidder Peabody, 119
King, Clarence, 57
Knights of the Dagger, 21
Kohlberg, Kravis, Roberts &
Company, 127–28
Kreuger, Ivar, 79
Kuhn, Loeb, 31, 40, 45

Lamont, Thomas, 85–86
Lapham, Lewis, 93
Lee, Higginson, 119
Lewis, Michael, 90
Liar's Poker (Lewis), 90, 132
Lincoln, Abraham, 5, 56
Lippard, George, 148–49
Livermore, Jesse, 80
Livingston, Philip, 13
Lloyd, Henry Demarest, 32
Long, Huey, 48–49

Madison, James, 15–16, 18–19
Mather, Cotton, 143–44
McCabe, James D., 111
McClellan, George B., 56, 57
McKinley, William H., 24, 25, 39
Meehan, Michael, 79–80
Mellon, Andrew, 130
Melville, Herman, 68, 76, 170
merger movement: in the 1980s,
129; at the turn of the century,
39, 119–20
Merrill, Charles, 8
Merrill Lynch, 8
Milken, Michael, 6, 9, 51–52, 90,
104, 124–25, 126, 127, 128–29,
170

Mitchell, "Sunshine Charlie,"
49–50, 53, 82
Money Trust, 42–46, 49
Morgan, J. P., 4, 6, 9, 38, 110,
129–30, 161, 167; adulation of,
115–22, 126; as aristocrat, 39,
40–42, 44–45; death of, 45–46.
See also House of Morgan
Morgan, Jack, 50–51, 80
Myers, Gustavus, 152

Napoleon, mystique surrounding,
100–101, 104
Nast, Thomas, 163–64
National City Bank, 49
national debt: and fears of aristoc-
racy, 17–19; Hamilton's plan for,
14–16, 20
Netscape Communications Corpo-
ration, 87–88
New York by Gaslight (Foster), 65,
148
New York Stock Exchange, 64, 83
Northern Pacific Railroad, 72–73
Northern Securities Company, 40,
41
Noyes, Alexander Dana, 152

Other People's Money (play and film),
132

pension funds, 177
Phillips, Kevin, 171–72
Pintard, John, 21–22, 146
Politics of Rich and Poor (Phillips),
171–72
Ponzi, Charles, 5, 78–79
Populist Party, 117

Public Utility Holding Company Act, 49
Pujo, Arsène, 42, 44
Pulitzer, Joseph, 25
Pullman, George, 37
Pullman Strike of *1894*, 37

Quaker City; or, The Monks of Monk Hall (Lippard), 148–49
Qwest Communications, 91–92

railroads: Morgan's innovations to, 117–18; speculation involving, 71–76, 118
Raskob, John Jakob, 81, 85
RCA, 81
Reagan era, 52
religious fundamentalism, 168–69
Reynolds, George M., 44
Robinson, Richard P., 146
Rockefeller, John D., 42
Roosevelt, Franklin Delano, 4, 46–48, 80, 83–84
Roosevelt, Theodore, 39–41, 47
Rothschild, Baron, 57
Rothschild family, 136

Sage, Russell, 30, 100, 115
Sarbanes-Oxley Bill, 92–93
Schiff, Jacob, 45
Schuyler, Elizabeth, 14–15
Schuyler, Philip, 14–15
Schwab, Charles, 81
Second Bank of the United States, 149
Securities and Exchange Commission, 49
securities laws, 49, 92–93

Seligman, Henry, 56
Seligman Brothers, 119
Sherman Anti-trust Act, 40
Silk Stocking Regiment, 123–24
Slack, Silent John, 55–58
Smith, Ben, 79
Social Darwinism, 35, 112–13
Social Security, privatization of, 93–94, 172
social upheaval, during the late nineteenth century, 36–38
speculation: as gambling, 144; growth of, 61–63; investment pools, 81–82; involving railroads, 71–76, 118. *See also* confidence men
speculators, 107–9. *See also* confidence men; Duer, William; Fisk, "Jubilee Jim"; Gould, Jay; Kennedy, Joseph; Kreuger, Ivar; Livermore, Jesse; Meehan, Michael; Mitchell, "Sunshine Charlie"
Spencer, Herbert, 113
Standard Oil, 42
Steichen, Edward, 110
Steinberg, Saul, 127
stock market crash. *See* Crash of 1929
Stowe, Harriet Beecher, 37
Sumner, William Graham, 35, 113
Sun Tzu, 126

Temple University, 161
Thompson, William, 66–68
Tiffany, Charles, 57
Tocqueville, Alexis de, 127
Tumulty, Joseph, 81

Index

Twain, Mark, 26, 55, 60, 76–78
Tweed, Boss, 164
Tyco, 91–92

Union Pacific Railroad, 77
United States of America, relation
with Europe, 122–23
Untermeyer, Samuel, 44–45

Vanderbilt, Cornelius, 5–6, 30, 105,
115; monument to, 99–100, 160;
mythologizing of, 97–100, 111,
112; and railroad speculation,
74–76

Wall Street: ambivalence toward,
23; anti-Semitism directed at,
136, 140–42; books about, 90,
132, 169–70; criticisms of, 33;
democratizing of, 8; fears regarding, 24; in fiction, 26, 55, 77–78,
86, 89–90, 112–15, 145, 147,
148–49, 157–58, 164–66; in
film, 8, 88–89, 125, 132; as
gambling venue, 139–40, 146,
163, 176; magazines devoted to,
125; political challenges to, 34,
166–68, 171; press coverage of,
147–49; public perceptions of,

92–95, 156–57, 169–73, 175–80;
symbolic associations with, 1–3,
177; uncertainty inherent in,
106–8; as viewed by religious
leaders, 161–63. *See also* aris-
tocracy; confidence men; hero;
immoralists
Wall Street (film), 8, 89, 125
Warner, Charles Dudley, 26, 55,
77
Washington, George, 14, 17–18,
145
Wasserstein, Bruce, 127
Watson, Tom, 25–26
wealth, as moral issue, 154–56, 162
Wealth Tax Act, 49
Welch, Jack, 124
Wharton, Edith, 169
Whitney, George, 82–83
Whitney, Richard, 82–84
Wilkinson, William, 46
Wilson, Edmund, 49
Wilson, Woodrow, 43–44, 81
Wolfe, Tom, 132, 170
Wood, Ferdinand, 71
World War I, 123–24
WorldCom, 91–92

Yerkes, Charles, 104